Green **Line 1**

Vokabellernheft

Ernst Klett Verlag
Stuttgart • Leipzig

Vorwort

Dieses Vokabellernheft im Taschenformat enthält alle Wörter und Wendungen aus *Green Line* 1. Du kannst es überall hin mitnehmen, um Vokabeln zu lernen und zu wiederholen.
Am besten hast du beim Lernen immer einen Bleistift zur Hand. Damit markierst du Wörter und Wendungen, die dir besondere Schwierigkeiten bereiten. Diese kannst du dann in regelmäßigen Abständen immer wieder durchgehen.
Am Ende jeder Unit findest du zahlreiche Übungen, mit denen du das Gelernte ordnen und wiederholen kannst. Die Übungen helfen dir auch bei der Vorbereitung auf Vokabeltests.

Viel Spaß wünscht dir dein *Green-Line*-Team!

LERNTIPP

Lerne Vokabeln mündlich und schriftlich, denn zwei Kanäle sind zwei Lernchancen!

Decke zunächst die rechte Vokabelspalte mit den deutschen Bezeichnungen ab und übersetze die englischen Wörter / Sätze. Decke anschließend die linke Vokabelseite mit den englischen Wörtern / Sätzen zu und übersetze sie schriftlich.

Zoom-in Time for Greenwich

zoom-in [zu:m'ɪn]	Heranzoomen, Heranfahren
time [taɪm]	Zeit
for [fɔ:; fə]	für
24-hour [twentiˌfɔ:‿'aʊə]	24-Stunden-
clock [klɒk]	Uhr
bus pl. **buses** [bʌs; bʌsɪz]	Bus
to [tu:; tʊ; tə]	nach, zu, in
let's listen [lets 'lɪsn]	lass(t) uns zuhören
let's (= let us) [lets; let‿'ʌs]	lass(t) uns
to **listen** ['lɪsn]	zuhören
sound [saʊnd]	Geräusch
to **point** [pɔɪnt]	zeigen

Unit 1 Thomas Tallis School

Check-in

check-in ['tʃekɪn]	Einchecken
pick-up ['pɪkʌp]	Pick-up, Kleintransporter
to **pick up** [pɪk‿'ʌp]	abholen, mitnehmen
unit ['ju:nɪt]	Lektion, Kapitel, Einheit
Thomas Tallis [ˌtɒməs 'tælɪs]	
school [sku:l]	Schule
Hello. [hel'əʊ]	Hallo.

My name is … . [maɪ ˈneɪm‿ɪz]	Ich heiße …
I'm (= I am) [aɪm; ˌaɪ ˈæm]	ich bin
eleven [ɪˈlevn]	elf
from [frɒm; frəm]	aus, von
in [ɪn]	in
London [ˈlʌndən]	
a, an [ə; ən]	ein/-e
pupil [ˈpjuːpl]	Schüler, Schülerin
at [æt; ət]	in, auf, bei, an
twelve [twelv]	zwölf
too [tuː]	auch
this [ðɪs]	diese/-r/-s
new [njuː]	neu
year [jɪə]	Jahr; Jahrgangsstufe, Klasse, Schuljahr
seven [ˈsevn]	sieben
tiny [ˈtaɪni]	klein, winzig
mouse [maʊs]	Maus
one [wʌn]	eins
and [ænd; ənd]	und
home [həʊm]	Zuhause
What's your name? [wɒts jɔː ˈneɪm]	Wie heißt du?
How old are you? [haʊ‿ˈəʊld‿ɑː ˈjuː]	Wie alt bist du?
Where are you from? [ˌweər‿ə jə ˈfrɒm]	Woher kommst du?
How to … [ˈhaʊ tə]	Wie man …
to **say hello** [seɪ helˈəʊ]	jemanden begrüßen
to **say** [seɪ]	sagen
useful [ˈjuːsfl]	nützlich, hilfreich
phrase [freɪz]	Satz, Redewendung
ten [ten]	zehn
Listening [ˈlɪsnɪŋ]	*hier:* Hörverstehensübung
phone number [ˈfəʊn ˌnʌmbə]	Telefonnummer
number [ˈnʌmbə]	Nummer, Hausnummer; Zahl

Numbers 1–12		
1 one [wʌn]	**5 five** [faɪv]	**9 nine** [naɪn]
2 two [tu:]	**6 six** [sɪks]	**10 ten** [ten]
3 three [θri:]	**7 seven** ['sevn]	**11 eleven** [ɪ'levn]
4 four [fɔ:]	**8 eight** [eɪt]	**12 twelve** [twelv]

mobile ['məʊbaɪl]	Handy, Mobiltelefon
ring! ring! [rɪŋ]	klingeling!
or [ɔ:]	oder
to **write** [raɪt]	schreiben
the [ðə; ði]	der, die (*auch pl.*), das
Hands on [hændz‿'ɒn]	Pack's an!
folder ['fəʊldə]	Ordner, Mappe
to **start** [stɑ:t]	anfangen, beginnen
English ['ɪŋglɪʃ]	Englisch
word bank ['wɜ:d ˌbæŋk]	Wortsammlung
word [wɜ:d]	Wort
to **know** [nəʊ]	kennen; wissen
primary school ['praɪmri ˌsku:l]	Grundschule
more [mɔ:]	mehr; weitere
about [ə'baʊt]	über
yourself [jɔ:'self]	dich selbst

Language 1: A new friend

language ['læŋgwɪdʒ]	Sprache
meeting people ['mi:tɪŋ ˌpi:pl]	Leute kennenlernen, Leute treffen
friend [frend]	Freund
but [bʌt]	aber
it's (= it is) [ɪts; ɪt‿'ɪz]	es ist
big [bɪg]	groß
here's (= here is) [hɪəz; hɪə‿'ɪz]	hier ist
he's (= he is) [hi:z; hi:‿'ɪz]	er ist
she's (= she is) [ʃi:z; ʃi:‿'ɪz]	sie ist
that's (= that is) [ðæts; ðæt‿'ɪz]	das ist
Mrs ['mɪsɪz]	Frau *(Anrede)*

tutor ['tju:tə]	Klassenlehrer, Klassenlehrerin
German teacher ['dʒɜ:mən ˌti:tʃə]	Deutschlehrer, Deutschlehrerin
so [səʊ]	also, folglich, deshalb
you're (= you are) [jɔ:; ju:‿'ɑ:]	du bist; ihr seid; Sie sind
tutor group ['tju:tə gru:p]	Klasse *(in einer englischen Schule)*
favourite ['feɪvrɪt]	Lieblings-
sport [spɔ:t]	Sport, Sportart
football ['fʊtbɔ:l]	Fußball
goal [gəʊl]	Tor
England ['ɪŋglənd]	
shoe [ʃu:]	Schuh
thank you ['θæŋk ju]	danke
Mr ['mɪstə]	Herr *(Anrede)*
caretaker ['keəteɪkə]	Hausmeister, Hausmeisterin
scary ['skeəri]	beängstigend, unheimlich
example [ɪg'zɑ:mpl]	Beispiel
go on, please [gəʊ‿'ɒn pli:z]	Mach / Macht bitte weiter.
please [pli:z]	bitte
game [geɪm]	Spiel
wrong [rɒŋ]	falsch
right [raɪt]	richtig
order ['ɔ:də]	Reihenfolge
tip [tɪp]	Tipp, Ratschlag
Your turn. ['jɔ: tɜ:n]	Du bist dran.

Language 2: Sam

long [lɒŋ]	lang
short [ʃɔ:t]	kurz
form [fɔ:m]	Form
are [ɑ:]	bist, sind, seid
we [wi:; wi]	wir
classroom ['klɑ:srʊm]	Klassenzimmer
Yes, we are. [jes wi‿'ɑ:]	Ja, das sind wir.
isn't (=is not) [ɪznt; ɪz‿'nɒt]	ist nicht
sure [ʃɔ:; ʃʊə]	sicher

room [ru:m]	Zimmer, Raum
No, he isn't. [ˌnəʊ hi‿ˈɪznt]	Nein, ist er nicht.
who's (= who is) [hu:z; hu:‿ˈɪz]	wer ist
nice [naɪs]	nett, sympathisch
always [ˈɔ:lweɪz]	immer
He's late. [hi:z ˈleɪt]	Er kommt zu spät. / Er ist spät dran.
You're lucky. [jʊə ˈlʌki]	Du hast Glück. / Ihr habt Glück.
not [nɒt]	nicht
aren't (= are not) [ɑ:nt; ɑ:‿ˈnɒt]	bist / sind / seid nicht
they [ðeɪ]	sie
Good morning. [gʊd ˈmɔ:nɪŋ]	Guten Morgen.
girl [gɜ:l]	Mädchen
boy [bɔɪ]	Junge
What's up? [wɒts‿ˈʌp]	Was ist los?
I'm sorry. [aɪm ˈsɒrɪ]	Es tut mir leid.
bag [bæg]	Tasche
with [wɪð]	mit
book [bʊk]	Buch
mum [mʌm]	Mama
people *(pl.)* [ˈpi:pl]	Leute *(pl.)*, Menschen *(pl.)*
to **put in** [pʊt ˈɪn]	einsetzen
on [ɒn]	auf; an
page [peɪdʒ]	Seite
her [hɜ:]	ihr/-e
diary [ˈdaɪəri]	Tagebuch
so [səʊ]	so
very [ˈveri]	sehr
grammar [ˈgræmə]	Grammatik
to **look at** [ˈlʊk‿æt]	anschauen, ansehen
picture [ˈpɪktʃə]	Bild
to **make** [meɪk]	machen, bilden
sentence [ˈsentəns]	Satz
question [ˈkwestʃən]	Frage
answer [ˈɑ:nsə]	Antwort

Language 3: The schoolbag

school things *(pl.)*	['sku:l ˌθɪŋz]	Schulsachen *(pl.)*
schoolbag	['sku:lbæg]	Schultasche
pencil-case	['pensl keɪs]	Federmäppchen
pen	[pen]	Füller
pencil	['pensl]	Bleistift
rubber	['rʌbə]	Radiergummi
ruler	['ru:lə]	Lineal
exercise book	['eksəsaɪz ˌbʊk]	Heft
apple	['æpl]	Apfel
to **copy**	['kɒpi]	abschreiben, abmalen
grid	[grɪd]	Raster, Tabelle
to **listen for**	['lɪsn fə]	heraushören
to **fill in**	[fɪl‿'ɪn]	ausfüllen
sound	[saʊnd]	Laut
list	[lɪst]	Liste
to **play**	[pleɪ]	spielen

Numbers 13–100

13 thirteen [θɜ:'ti:n]	**20 twenty** ['twenti]	**40 forty** ['fɔ:ti]
14 fourteen [fɔ:'ti:n]	**21 twenty-one** ['twenti'wʌn]	**50 fifty** ['fɪfti]
15 fifteen [fɪf'ti:n]	**22 twenty-two** ['twenti'tu:]	**60 sixty** ['sɪksti]
16 sixteen [sɪks'ti:n]	**23 twenty-three** ['twentiθri:]	**70 seventy** ['sevnti]
17 seventeen [sevn'ti:n]	**24 twenty-four** ['twenti'fɔ:]	**80 eighty** ['eɪti]
18 eighteen [eɪ'ti:n]	…	**90 ninety** ['naɪnti]
19 nineteen [nain'ti:n]	**30 thirty** ['θɜ:ti]	**100 one hundred** [wʌn'hʌndrəd]

plural	['plʊərl]	Plural, Mehrzahl
alphabet	['ælfəbet]	Alphabet
to **clap**	[klæp]	klatschen
lesson	['lesn]	Unterrichtsstunde
to **shout**	[ʃaʊt]	rufen, schreien
to **do**	[du:; də; du]	machen, tun
to **spell**	[spel]	buchstabieren

The alphabet

a [eɪ]	**g** [dʒi:]	**m** [em]	**s** [es]	**y** [waɪ]
b [bi:]	**h** [eɪtʃ]	**n** [en]	**t** [ti:]	**z** [zed]
c [si:]	**i** [ai]	**o** [əʊ]	**u** [ju:]	
d [di:]	**j** [dʒeɪ]	**p** [pi:]	**v** [vi:]	
e [i:]	**k** [keɪ]	**q** [kju:]	**w** ['dʌblju:]	
f [ef]	**l** [el]	**r** [ɑ:]	**x** [eks]	

Language 4: The classroom

window ['wɪndəʊ]	Fenster
chair [tʃeə]	Stuhl
board [bɔ:d]	Tafel; Brett
poster ['pəʊstə]	Poster
door [dɔ:]	Tür
wall [wɔ:l]	Wand, Mauer
table ['teɪbl]	Tisch
cupboard ['kʌbəd]	Schrank
desk [desk]	Schreibtisch
there's (= there is) [ðeəz; ðeə‿'ɪz]	da ist, dort ist; es gibt
there are [ðeər‿'ɑ:]	da sind, es gibt
crisp [krɪsp]	Kartoffelchip
under ['ʌndə]	unter
behind [bɪ'haɪnd]	hinter
chocolate ['tʃɒklət]	Schokolade
in [ɪn]	in, im
to **phone** [fəʊn]	anrufen
in front of [ɪn 'frʌnt‿əv]	vor
to **use** [ju:z]	benutzen, verwenden, gebrauchen
classroom phrases *(pl.)* ['klɑ:srʊm ˌfreɪzɪz]	Redewendungen für den Unterricht
in English [ɪn‿'ɪŋglɪʃ]	auf Englisch
Sorry I'm late. [ˌsɒri‿aɪm 'leɪt]	Tut mir leid, dass ich zu spät komme.

What's for homework, please? [wɒts fə 'həʊmwɜːk ˌpliːz]	Was haben wir als Hausaufgabe auf, bitte?
Can I go to the toilet, please? [kən‿aɪ ˌgəʊ tə ðə 'tɔɪlət pliːz]	Kann ich bitte zur Toilette gehen?
Sit down, please. [sɪt 'daʊn pliːz]	Setz dich / Setzt euch bitte hin.
You're welcome. [jɔː 'welkəm]	Bitte schön. / Nichts zu danken. / Gern geschehen.
goodbye [gʊd'baɪ]	auf Wiedersehen
bye [baɪ]	tschüss
now [naʊ]	jetzt, nun, gerade

Text: No problem!

text [tekst]	Text
no [nəʊ]	kein/-e
problem ['prɒbləm]	Problem
eatery ['iːtri]	Kantine, Restaurant
lunchtime ['lʌnʃtaɪm]	Mittagszeit, Mittagspause
cafeteria [kæfə'tɪəriə]	Cafeteria
Look! [lʊk]	Schau mal! / Sieh mal!
joke [dʒəʊk]	Witz
letter ['letə]	Buchstabe
easy ['iːzi]	leicht, einfach
boring ['bɔːrɪŋ]	langweilig
terrible ['terəbl]	schrecklich, schlimm, furchtbar
playground ['pleɪgraʊnd]	Schulhof; Spielplatz
she is good at [ʃi‿ɪz 'gʊd‿ət]	sie ist gut in / bei …
to **watch out** [wɒtʃ 'aʊt]	aufpassen
ball [bɔːl]	Ball
tree [triː]	Baum
dialogue ['daɪəlɒg]	Dialog
to **complete** [kəm'pliːt]	vervollständigen
to **put** [pʊt]	stellen, setzen, legen
them [ðem; ðəm]	sie

polite [pəˈlaɪt]	höflich
you're wrong [jɔː ˈrɒŋ]	du hast Unrecht, du irrst dich

Wordwise

wordwise [ˈwɜːdwaɪz]	„wortschlau", „wortgewandt"
word web [ˈwɜːd web]	Wortnetz
vocabulary [vəˈkæbjəlri]	Vokabular, Wortschatz
skill [skɪl]	Fertigkeit
to **find** [faɪnd]	finden
good [gʊd]	gut
adjective [ˈædʒɪktɪv]	Adjektiv, Eigenschaftswort
other [ˈʌðə]	andere/-r/-s, weitere/-r/-s

Check-out

check-out [ˈtʃekaʊt]	Auschecken
What is missing? [ˌwɒt‿ɪz ˈmɪsɪŋ]	Was fehlt?
different [ˈdɪfrnt]	anders, unterschiedlich

1 Greetings

Wie begrüßt man jemanden und wie verabschiedet man sich?

Zur Begrüßung	**Zum Abschied**
______________________	______________________
______________________	______________________
______________________	

2 Prepositions

Wo ist Tom? Notiere die Präpositionen.

1. ______________________

2. ______________________

3. ______________________

4. ______________________

3 Questions

Welche Fragen kannst du stellen, um mehr über jemanden zu erfahren?

1. Wie heißt du? ______________________
2. Wie alt bist du? ______________________
3. Woher kommst du? ______________________

4 Short forms and long forms: *to be*

short form	long form
I'm	1.
2.	you are
he's	3.
4.	she is
it's	5.
6.	we are
you're	7.
8.	they are

5 Your turn

Was kannst du über dich selbst auf Englisch sagen?

1. Mein Name ist … ______________________________
2. Ich bin … Jahre alt. ______________________________
3. Ich komme aus … ______________________________
4. Meine Telefonnummer ist … ______________________________

6 Numbers 1–12

Welche Zahlen sind in der Schlange versteckt?
Markiere sie zunächst und schreibe sie anschließend auf.

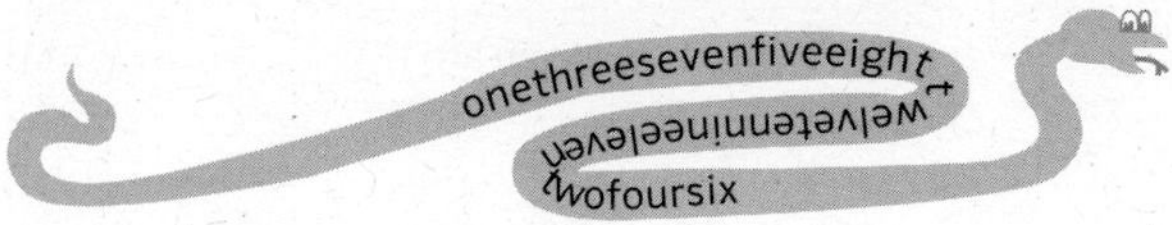

____

____

____

7 Numbers 13–100

Ergänze die Lücken.

1. fourteen, fifteen, ____________________
2. nineteen, ____________________, twenty-one
3. twenty-three, twenty-five, ____________________
4. forty, ____________________, forty-four
5. sixty, seventy, ____________________

8 Alphabet

Kennst du englische Wörter, die mit diesen Buchstaben beginnen?

1. S____________________
2. A____________________
3. N____________________
4. D____________________
5. W____________________
6. I____________________
7. C____________________
8. H____________________

9 Question words

Du hast vier neue Fragewörter gelernt. Ergänze sie in den Fragen.

1. ____________________'s your name?
2. ____________________ are you from?
3. ____________________ old are you?
4. ____________________'s the caretaker at TTS?

10 Words for pictures

Wie heißen die Dinge?

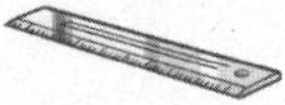

1. ______________________

2. ______________________

3. ______________________

4. ______________________

5. ______________________

6. ______________________

11 Adjectives

In dieser Unit hast du einige Adjektive gelernt. Welche? Notiere so viele wie möglich.

old, ______________________

____

____

____

12 Verbs

Wie heißt das Verb? Ergänze die fehlenden Buchstaben.

1. l i ___ ___ e n
2. w ___ i ___ e
3. s p ___ l l
4. m a ___ e
5. s h ___ u t
6. f i ___ l i ___

13 *a* or *an*?

1. _______ apple
2. _______ ruler
3. _______ old pencil
4. _____ sandwich
5. _____ exercise
6. _____ new pen

14 In the classroom

Welche Substantive verstecken sich im Buchstabensalat?

1. NIWWOD _______________
2. BPOCUDAR _____________
3. OORD __________________
4. BAELT __________________
5. SEKD ___________________
6. RAHCI _________________

15 What word?

Welches Wort verbirgt sich hinter der Lautschrift?

1. [pli:z] _______________
2. [ku:l] _______________
3. ['pensl] _______________
4. ['letə] _______________

LERNTIPP

Verbinde – wenn möglich – in deinem Kopf die Vokabel mit einem Bild!

sofa + 

Pick-up A Home sweet home

home sweet home ['həʊm ˌswi:t 'həʊm]	trautes Heim *(Sprichwort)*
sweet [swi:t]	süß
purple ['pɜ:pl]	violett, lila
grey [greɪ]	grau
green [gri:n]	grün
black [blæk]	schwarz
white [waɪt]	weiß
pink [pɪŋk]	rosa, pink
red [red]	rot
blue [blu:]	blau
orange ['ɒrɪndʒ]	orange
brown [braʊn]	braun
yellow ['jeləʊ]	gelb
card [kɑ:d]	Karte, Spielkarte
per [pɜ:; pə]	pro
to **hold up** [həʊld 'ʌp]	hochhalten
correct [kə'rekt]	richtig
colour ['kʌlə]	Farbe
open ['əʊpn]	geöffnet, offen; aufgeschlagen
to **ask** [ɑ:sk]	fragen
then [ðen]	dann, danach
to **close** [kləʊz]	schließen, zumachen
to **answer** ['ɑ:nsə]	(be)antworten
kitchen ['kɪtʃɪn]	Küche
living room ['lɪvɪŋ ru:m]	Wohnzimmer
bathroom ['bɑ:θru:m]	Bad(ezimmer)
bedroom ['bedru:m]	Schlafzimmer

rhyme [raɪm]	Reim
bed [bed]	Bett
sofa ['səʊfə]	Sofa, Couch
funny ['fʌni]	lustig, witzig
house [haʊs]	Haus
TV [ˌtiː'viː]	Fernseher
to **learn by heart** [ˌlɜːn baɪ 'hɑːt]	auswendig lernen
to **describe** [dɪ'skraɪb]	beschreiben
like this [laɪk 'ðɪs]	so, auf diese Weise
furniture ['fɜːnɪtʃə]	Möbel
dream [driːm]	Traum
to **talk to** [tɔːk tə]	sprechen mit, reden mit
to **draw** [drɔː]	zeichnen
his [hɪz]	sein/-e
family ['fæmli]	Familie
mother ['mʌðə]	Mutter
grandfather ['grænˌfɑːðə]	Großvater
grandad ['grændæd]	Opa
brother ['brʌðə]	Bruder
sister ['sɪstə]	Schwester
father ['fɑːðə]	Vater
dad [dæd]	Papa, Vati
grandmother ['grænˌmʌðə]	Großmutter
grandma ['grænmɑː]	Oma
happy ['hæpi]	glücklich, fröhlich
What colour are … ? [wɒt 'kʌlə‿ɑː]	Welche Farbe haben … ?

Unit 2 At home in Greenwich

at home [æt 'həʊm]	zu Hause

Check-in

parents *(pl.)* ['peərnts]	Eltern
half-sister ['hɑːfˌsɪstə]	Halbschwester

step-father ['stepˌfɑːðə]	Stiefvater
our [aʊə; ɑː]	unser/-e
flat [flæt]	Wohnung
road [rəʊd]	Straße
over ['əʊvə]	über
computer shop [kəm'pjuːtə ˌʃɒp]	Computergeschäft
shop [ʃɒp]	Geschäft, Laden
its [ɪts]	sein
small [smɔːl]	klein
Nasreen and I are … [nʌs'riːn‿ənd‿aɪ‿ɑː]	Nasreen und ich sind …
only child [ˌəʊnli 'tʃaɪld]	Einzelkind
child pl. **children** ['tʃaɪld; 'tʃɪldrn]	Kind
cat [kæt]	Katze
tiger ['taɪgə]	Tiger
interested in ['ɪntrəstɪd]	interessiert an
mice *(pl.)* [maɪs]	Mäuse *(pl.)*
garden ['gɑːdn]	Garten
shed [ʃed]	Schuppen, Gartenhäuschen
drums *(pl.)* [drʌmz]	Schlagzeug
chemistry set ['kemɪstri set]	Chemiekasten
to **match** [mætʃ]	zuordnen
dog [dɒg]	Hund
photo ['fəʊtəʊ]	Foto
to **listen to** ['lɪsn tə]	jemandem zuhören
why [waɪ]	warum
upstairs [ʌp'steəz]	oben, im Obergeschoss
downstairs [daʊn'steəz]	unten, im Untergeschoss

Language 1: Sam's family tree

nationality [ˌnæʃn'æləti]	Nationalität
family tree ['fæmli ˌtriː]	Familienstammbaum
married to ['mærid tə]	verheiratet mit
aunt [ɑːnt]	Tante
uncle ['ʌŋkl]	Onkel

divorced from [dɪˈvɔːst frəm]	geschieden von
cousin [ˈkʌzn]	Cousin, Cousine
European [jʊərəˈpiːən]	europäisch, aus Europa; Europäer/-in
Polish [ˈpəʊlɪʃ]	polnisch, aus Polen; Polnisch
because [bɪˈkɒz]	weil, da
Poland [ˈpəʊlənd]	Polen
English [ˈɪŋglɪʃ]	englisch, aus England
Greek [griːk]	griechisch, aus Griechenland; Griechisch
today [təˈdeɪ]	heute
lunch [lʌnʃ]	Mittagessen
Italian [ɪˈtæliən]	italienisch, aus Italien; Italienisch
your [jɔː]	Ihr(e)
their [ðeə]	ihr, ihre *(Plural)*
to **tell** [tel]	erzählen, sagen
Germany [ˈdʒɜːməni]	Deutschland
Russia [ˈrʌʃə]	Russland
Russian [ˈrʌʃn]	russisch, aus Russland; Russisch
Greece [griːs]	Griechenland
Italy [ˈɪtli]	Italien
Turkey [ˈtɜːki]	Türkei
Turkish [ˈtɜːkɪʃ]	türkisch, aus der Türkei; Türkisch
Spain [speɪn]	Spanien
Spanish [ˈspænɪʃ]	spanisch, aus Spanien; Spanisch

Language 2: Emma, you're in big trouble!

saying what you've got [ˈseɪɪŋ ˌwɒt jʊv ˈgɒt]	sagen, was jemand hat
You're in big trouble. [jɔːr‿ɪn ˈbɪg ˌtrʌbl]	Du steckst in großen Schwierigkeiten.
she has got [ʃi həz ˈgɒt]	sie hat …
only [ˈəʊnli]	nur, bloß

wardrobe ['wɔ:drəʊb]	Kleiderschrank
a lot of [ə 'lɒt‿əv]	viel/-e, eine Menge
outside [ˌaʊt'saɪd]	außen, draußen, im Freien; außerhalb
She is in a hurry. [ˌʃi‿ɪz ɪn ə 'hʌri]	Sie hat es eilig.
to **look** [lʊk]	nachschauen, suchen
magazine [ˌmægə'zi:n]	Zeitschrift
second ['seknd]	Sekunde
maybe ['meɪbi]	vielleicht
Here it is. [ˌhɪər‿ɪt‿'ɪz]	Hier ist es.
dirty ['dɜ:ti]	dreckig, schmutzig
What a mess! [wɒt‿ə 'mes]	Was für eine Unordnung!
later ['leɪtə]	später
just [dʒʌst]	nur
silly ['sɪli]	albern, dumm
well [wel]	tja, nun
to **sort out** [sɔ:t 'aʊt]	klären, regeln
her own room [hər‿ˌəʊn 'ru:m]	ihr eigenes Zimmer
car [kɑ:]	Auto

Language 3: Rules for our room

rule [ru:l]	Regel
can't [kɑ:nt; 'kænɒt]	nicht können
CD [ˌsi:'di:]	CD
How can I do my homework? ['haʊ kən‿aɪ ˌdu: maɪ 'həʊmwɜ:k]	Wie soll ich meine Hausaufgaben machen?
music ['mju:zɪk]	Musik
idea [aɪ'dɪə]	Idee
to **help** [help]	helfen
to **take turns** [teɪk 'tɜ:nz]	sich abwechseln
Don't use … [dəʊnt 'ju:s]	Benutze nicht …
quiet [kwaɪət]	leise, ruhig, still
when [wen]	wenn, als
to **play** [pleɪ]	(ab)spielen *(CD, Radio etc.)*
to **take** [teɪk]	(weg)nehmen

the same [ðə 'seɪm]	der- / die- / dasselbe, der / die / das Gleiche
to **open** ['əʊpn]	öffnen, aufmachen
to **have a party** [hæv ə 'pɑ:ti]	eine Party feiern
great [greɪt]	toll, großartig
Emma is good with … [ˌemə ɪz 'gʊd wɪð]	Emma kann mit … gut umgehen
rubber ball [ˌrʌbə 'bɔ:l]	Gummiball
revision [rɪ'vɪʒn]	Wiederholung
to [tu:; tʊ; tə]	an
to **say hello to** [seɪ hel'əʊ tə]	grüßen, Grüße ausrichten
I'm with … [aɪm 'wɪð]	Ich bin bei …

Text: Terry's shed

before [bɪ'fɔ:]	bevor
one Saturday afternoon [wʌn 'sætədeɪ ˌɑ:ftə'nu:n]	an einem Samstag Nachmittag
busy (with) ['bɪzi ˌwɪð]	beschäftigt (mit)
project ['prɒdʒekt]	Projekt
slow [sləʊ]	langsam
he is fed up (with) [hi: ɪz fed 'ʌp wɪð]	er ist sauer, er hat die Nase voll (von)
to **finish** ['fɪnɪʃ]	(be)enden, fertig stellen
Nasreen is a pain. [nʌsˌri:n‿ɪz ə 'peɪn]	Nasreen geht mir auf die Nerven.
to **come over** [kʌm 'əʊvə]	herüberkommen, vorbeischauen
soon [su:n]	bald
thanks [θæŋks]	danke
to **stop** [stɒp]	aufhören, beenden
smoke [sməʊk]	Rauch
everywhere ['evriweə]	überall
smell [smel]	Geruch, Duft, Gestank
yuk [jʌk]	i, igitt
beautiful ['bju:tɪfl]	schön; wunderbar
crystal ['krɪstl]	Kristall
… is fun [ɪz 'fʌn]	… macht Spaß, … ist witzig

to **talk about** [tɔ:k ə'baʊt] sprechen über
to **sort** [sɔ:t] sortieren

Wordwise

group [gru:p] Gruppe
to **underline** [ˌʌndə'laɪn] unterstreichen

1 Colours

Welche Farben werden beigemischt?

1. red + blue = purple
2. blue + yellow = green
3. yellow + red = orange
4. black + whirte = grey

2 Rooms

Wie werden die Räume bezeichnet?

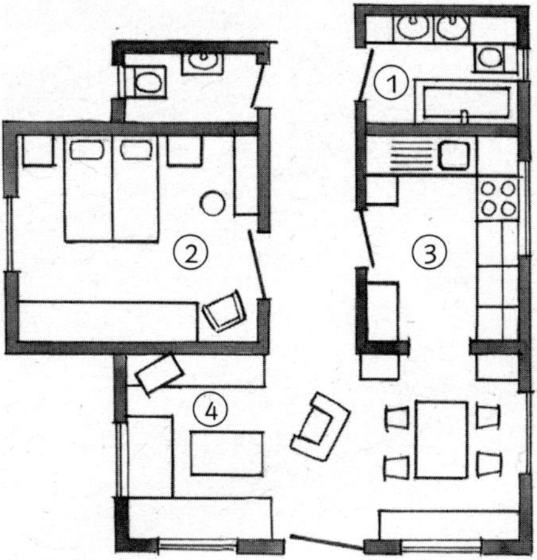

1. ______________________ 3. ______________________

2. ______________________ 4. ______________________

3 Furniture

Wie heißen die Möbelstücke? Sortiere die Buchstaben.

1. edb ______________ 4. ctpriue ______________

2. betla ______________ 5. faos ______________

3. trcpmeou ______________ 6. bcoudapr ______________

4 Families 1

Finde sechs „Familienwörter" im Wortgitter. Sie sind in beide Leserichtungen (vorwärts und rückwärts) versteckt. Schreibe sie anschließend auf.

P	D	S	A	T	O	D	A
D	O	A	M	J	P	G	R
S	D	A	D	N	A	R	G
A	M	O	N	T	I	E	S
V	B	R	A	N	E	H	I
Q	F	L	R	L	S	T	S
H	P	M	G	B	I	O	T
A	U	J	P	Y	C	R	E
M	G	M	A	H	G	B	R

____

____

____

____

____

____

5 Families 2

Wie heißen die Verwandten?

1. My father's sister = my ____________________
2. My mother's brother = my ____________________
3. My mother's or father's mother = my ____________________
4. My mother's or father's father = my ____________________

6 Opposites

Wie lautet das Gegenteil?

1. to start ↔ ______________________
2. to open ↔ ______________________
3. upstairs ↔ ______________________
4. married to ↔ ______________________

7 Nationalities

Ergänze die Nationalitäten.

1. Italy → ______________________
2. Greece → ______________________
3. Russia → ______________________
4. Turkey → ______________________
5. England → ______________________
6. Germany → ______________________

8 Possessive determiners

Notiere die englische Übersetzung.

1. mein, meine → ______________________
2. dein, deine; Ihr, Ihre → ______________________
3. sein, seine → ______________________
4. ihr, ihre (*Einzahl*) → ______________________
5. sein, seine → ______________________
6. unser, unsere → ______________________
7. euer, eure; Ihr, Ihre → ______________________
8. ihr, ihre (*Mehrzahl*) → ______________________

9 Words for pictures

Was ist abgebildet?

1. ______________________

2. ______________________

3. ______________________

4. ______________________

10 German words

Wie heißen diese Verben auf Deutsch?

1. to talk to ______________________
2. to answer ______________________
3. to describe ______________________
4. to tell ______________________
5. to ask ______________________
6. to shout ______________________
7. to say ______________________
8. to talk about ______________________

11 Describing people and things

Schreibe mindestens sechs Adjektive auf, mit denen du Personen oder Dinge beschreiben kannst.

sweet, ____

____

____

LERNTIPP

Mit der Lernsoftware zu *Green Line* 1 kannst du prima die Aussprache der Vokabeln trainieren: Du kannst dir einzelne Vokabeln vorsprechen lassen und sie anschließend nachsprechen. Mit dem Mikro kannst du deine eigene Aussprache aufnehmen.

Pick-up B Tom in Hobbyland

Hobbyland ['hɒbilænd]	Hobbyland
hobby pl. **hobbies** ['hɒbi; 'hɒbiz]	Hobby
land [lænd]	Land
to **ride** [raɪd]	reiten, fahren
bike [baɪk]	Fahrrad
to **watch** [wɒtʃ]	ansehen; beobachten
guitar [gɪ'tɑ:]	Gitarre
to **go swimming** [gəʊ 'swɪmɪŋ]	schwimmen gehen
to **swim** [swɪm]	schwimmen
to **read** [ri:d]	lesen
to **collect** [kə'lekt]	sammeln, einsammeln
role play ['rəʊl pleɪ]	Rollenspiel
Let's go! [lets 'gəʊ]	Lass(t) uns anfangen! / Lass(t) uns gehen!

days of the week *(pl.)* [ˌdeɪz‿ɒv ðə 'wi:k]	Wochentage *(pl.)*
day [deɪ]	Tag
week [wi:k]	Woche

Days of the week

Monday ['mʌndeɪ]	Montag
Tuesday ['tju:zdeɪ]	Dienstag
Wednesday ['wenzdeɪ]	Mittwoch
Thursday ['θɜ:zdeɪ]	Donnerstag
Friday ['fraɪdeɪ]	Freitag
Saturday ['sætədeɪ]	Samstag
Sunday ['sʌndeɪ]	Sonntag

Unit 3 Hobbies and clubs

club [klʌb]	Klub, Verein

Check-in

British ['brɪtɪʃ]	britisch
important [ɪm'pɔ:tnt]	wichtig
there [ðeə]	dorthin, dahin
free time ['fri: ˌtaɪm]	Freizeit
to **meet** [mi:t]	(sich) treffen
orchestra ['ɔ:kɪstrə]	Orchester
on Tuesdays [ɒn 'tju:zdeɪz]	dienstags
from … to ['frəm tə]	von … bis
pm [ˌpi:'em]	nachmittags *(Uhrzeit)*
cooking club ['kʊkɪŋ ˌklʌb]	Kochklub
am [ˌeɪ'em]	vormittags *(Uhrzeit)*
How about … ? [haʊ ə'baʊt]	Wie wäre es mit …
when [wen]	wann
at half past (three) [ət ˌhɑ:f pɑ:st 'θri:]	um halb (vier)
fine [faɪn]	in Ordnung, gut
Come on! [kʌm‿'ɒn]	Komm schon! / Komm jetzt!
See you there. [si: jə 'ðeə]	Wir sehen uns dort.
at the weekend [æt ðə ˌwi:k'end]	am Wochenende

cinema ['sɪnəmə]	Kino
film [fɪlm]	Film
boy band ['bɔɪ ˌbænd]	Boygroup
water ['wɔ:tə]	Wasser
o'clock [ə'klɒk]	Uhr (*Zeitangabe bei vollen Stunden*)
What time is it, please? [wɒt 'taɪm‿ɪz‿ɪt ˌpli:z]	Wie spät ist es, bitte?
to **tell the time** [ˌtel ðə 'taɪm]	die Uhr lesen
half [hɑ:f]	halb
quarter ['kwɔ:tə]	Viertel
past [pɑ:st]	nach *(bei Uhrzeitangaben)*
to [tu:; tʊ; tə]	vor *(bei Uhrzeitangaben)*
minute ['mɪnɪt]	Minute
at my house [ət 'maɪ haʊs]	bei mir zu Hause
town [taʊn]	Stadt

Language 1: A phone call from Grandma

daily ['deɪli]	täglich
routine [ru:'ti:n]	Routine
phone call ['fəʊn ˌkɔ:l]	(Telefon)Anruf
It's Mum here. [ɪts 'mʌm ˌhɪə]	Hier spricht Mama.
How are you? [ˌhaʊ‿ɑ: 'jə]	Wie geht es dir / Ihnen?
I'm fine. [ˌaɪm 'faɪn]	Mir geht es gut.
nice [naɪs]	schön, gut
to **get up** [get 'ʌp]	aufstehen
early ['ɜ:li]	früh
usually ['ju:ʒli]	gewöhnlich, normalerweise
every ['evri]	jede/-r/-s
What about … ? [wɒt‿ə'baʊt]	Was ist mit … ?
to **go home** [gəʊ 'həʊm]	nach Hause gehen
to **eat** [i:t]	essen
school day ['sku:l deɪ]	Schultag
never ['nevə]	nie, niemals
after ['ɑ:ftə]	nach; nachdem
often ['ɒfn]	oft, häufig
to **walk the dog** [wɔ:k ðə 'dɒg]	den Hund ausführen

to **walk** [wɔːk]	gehen *(zu Fuß)*
Lisa is great fun. ['liːsə ɪz 'greɪt ˌfʌn]	Lisa ist echt witzig.
sometimes ['sʌmtaɪmz]	manchmal
on TV [ɒn ˌtiː'viː]	im Fernsehen
in the evening [ɪn ði‿'iːvnɪŋ]	abends
to **fall asleep** [fɔːl‿ə'sliːp]	einschlafen
to **visit** ['vɪzɪt]	besuchen
us [ʌs; əs]	uns
dancing lessons *(pl.)* ['dɑːnsɪŋ ˌlesnz]	Tanzunterricht, Tanzstunden
first [fɜːst]	zuerst, als Erstes
again [ə'gen]	wieder, noch einmal, nochmal
box [bɒks]	Box, Kasten, Kästchen, Schachtel
this is … ['ðɪs‿ɪz]	hier ist …*(am Telefon)*

Language 2: Sam and Tiger

third person singular [θɜːd ˌpɜːsn 'sɪŋgjələ]	dritte Person Singular (Einzahl)
note [nəʊt]	Notiz, Nachricht
help [help]	Hilfe
tin [tɪn]	Dose, Büchse
cat food ['kæt ˌfuːd]	Katzenfutter
food [fuːd]	Essen, Nahrung, Nahrungsmittel
into ['ɪntə]	in (hinein)
next to ['nekst tə]	neben
chicken flavour ['tʃɪkɪn ˌfleɪvə]	Geschmacksrichtung „Hühnchen“
to **look** [lʊk]	aussehen
tasty ['teɪsti]	lecker
to **come in** [kʌm 'ɪn]	hereinkommen
hole [həʊl]	Loch
to **feed** [fiːd]	füttern
to **run away** [rʌn‿ə'weɪ]	weglaufen

to **run** [rʌn]	laufen, rennen
round the garden [raʊnd ðə ˈgɑːdn]	durch den ganzen Garten
neighbour [ˈneɪbə]	Nachbar, Nachbarin
after that [ˈɑːftə ðət]	danach
street [striːt]	Straße
There she is. [ˈðeə ʃi‿ɪz]	Da ist sie ja.
to **chase** [tʃeɪs]	verfolgen
finally [ˈfaɪnli]	schließlich, endlich, zum Schluss
to **go back** [gəʊ ˈbæk]	zurückgehen
to **wait** [weɪt]	warten
It's time to go home. [ɪts ˌtaɪm tə gəʊ ˈhəʊm]	Es ist Zeit, nach Hause zu gehen.
together [təˈgeðə]	zusammen; gemeinsam
to **like** [laɪk]	mögen
to **love** [lʌv]	lieben

Language 3: Sam's card trick

card trick [ˈkɑːd ˌtrɪk]	Kartenkunststück
those [ðəʊz]	diese (dort), jene
these [ðiːz]	diese (hier)
on the top [ɒn ðə ˈtɒp]	oben
on the bottom [ɒn ðə ˈbɒtəm]	unten
just [dʒʌst]	einfach
to **shuffle** [ˈʃʌfl]	mischen
to **hold** [həʊld]	halten, festhalten
to **bang** [bæŋ]	knallen, schlagen
He can't believe his eyes. [hi ˌkɑːnt bɪˌliːv hɪz ˈaɪz]	Er traut seinen Augen nicht.
to **work** [wɜːk]	funktionieren
nine of diamonds [naɪn‿əv ˈdaɪəməndz]	Karoneun *(beim Kartenspiel)*
eight of hearts [ˌeɪt‿əv ˈhɑːts]	Herzacht *(beim Kartenspiel)*
on top of [ɒn ˈtɒp‿əv]	auf … hinauf, oben (auf)
to **remember** [rɪˈmembə]	sich erinnern (an); denken an

to **forget** [fəˈget]	vergessen
which [wɪtʃ]	welche/-r/-s
to **show** [ʃəʊ]	zeigen
to **happen** [ˈhæpn]	passieren, geschehen
to **kick** [kɪk]	schießen; treten
linking sounds [ˌlɪŋkɪŋ ˈsaʊndz]	das Verbinden von Lauten
to **link** [lɪŋk]	verbinden

Text: Barker's story

story [ˈstɔːri]	Geschichte, Erzählung
pet [pet]	Haustier
to **wake up** [weɪk‿ˈʌp]	aufwecken; aufwachen
to **wash** [wɒʃ]	waschen
face [feɪs]	Gesicht
breakfast [ˈbrekfəst]	Frühstück
to **bark** [bɑːk]	bellen
to **take** [teɪk]	(mit)nehmen; bringen
to **teach** [tiːtʃ]	unterrichten, lehren, beibringen
to **bring** [brɪŋ]	(mit)bringen
to **throw** [θrəʊ]	werfen
me [miː]	mich; mir
to **get lost** [get ˈlɒst]	sich verirren
to **call** [kɔːl]	rufen, schreien
to **take out** [teɪk‿ˈaʊt]	ausführen
to **bark at** [ˈbɑːk‿ət]	anbellen
them [ðem; ðəm]	sie
drink [drɪŋk]	Getränk
to **fall over** [fɔːl ˈəʊvə]	umfallen, hinfallen
to **sleep** [sliːp]	schlafen
dog-tired [dɒgˈtaɪəd]	hundemüde
to **go to bed** [gəʊ tə ˈbed]	ins Bett gehen

Wordwise

mixed bag [ˌmɪkst ˈbæg] bunte Mischung
mixed [mɪkst] gemischt

Check-out

simple present [ˌsɪmpl ˈpreznt] Gegenwart, Präsens

1 Days of the week

Welche vier Wochentage haben ein „u"?

____

____

____

____

2 The other days

Schreibe nun die Wochentage ohne ein „u" auf.

____

____

____

3 Morning or afternoon?

Wie heißen die Abkürzungen bei Uhrzeiten?

1. vormittags ____________ 2. nachmittags ____________

4 Time snake

Welche Wörter sind in der Schlange versteckt?

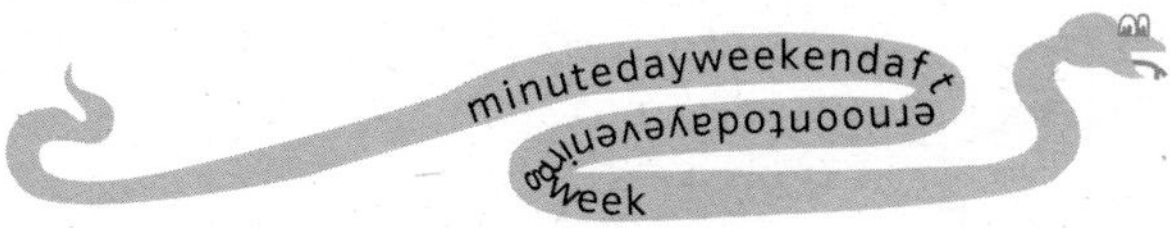

____

____

____

____

5 Time

Wie fragst du nach der Uhrzeit?

____

6 Time, again!

Schreibe die Uhrzeiten auf.

1. ______________________________

2. ______________________________

3. ______________________________

4. ______________________________

5. ______________________________

6. ______________________________

7 Adverbs

Wie heißen die Häufigkeitsadverbien?

1. s ___ ___ ___ t ___ ___ ___ s
2. o ___ ___ ___ ___
3. n ___ ___ ___ ___
4. u ___ ___ ___ ___ ___ ___
5. a ___ ___ ___ ___ ___

8 Sport

Welche Sportarten kennst du? Schreibe vier auf.

____

____

9 Verbs

Setze die Verben in der richtigen Form ein.

1. I ______________ (layp) the guitar.
2. He ______________ (tcawhse) a video.
3. She ______________ (eogs) swimming.
4. It ______________ (letsl) the time.
5. They ______________ (dire) bikes.
6. We ______________ (gisn) and

   ______________ (cndea) at the Drama Club.

10 Questions

Wie heißen die Fragen auf Deutsch?

1. What about your homework? ______________________

   ____

2. How are you? ______________________________

   ____

3. How about the cinema? ________________________

   ____

11 The simple present

Setze die Verben in der richtigen Form ein.

1. I walk → she ______________
2. they go → he ______________
3. we play → she ______________
4. you watch → he ______________

12 Words for pictures

Was ist abgebildet?

1. ______________________________

2. ______________________________

3. ______________________________

4. ______________________________

5. ______________________________

13 Verbs, again!

*Welches Verb passt – **fall**, **run**, **get** oder **wake**?*

1. to ______________ away
2. to ______________ up
3. to ______________ over
4. to ______________ up
5. to ______________ lost
6. to ______________ asleep

14 Missing letters

Setze die fehlenden Buchstaben ein.

1. e v ___ ___ ___ n g
2. t h ___ ___ w
3. n e i g h b ___ ___ r
4. ___ ___ o r y
5. h o b ___ ___
6. o r ___ ___ e s t ___ a
7. r ___ ___ d
8. w ___ l k the d ___ ___

15 Odd one out

Welches Wort tanzt aus der Reihe? Markiere es.

1.	football	basketball	breakfast
2.	often	today	always
3.	to love	to like	to link
4.	after	afternoon	evening
5.	bike	town	car
6.	quarter	half	early

LERNTIPP

Schreibe Wörter / Ausdrücke, die dir schwierig erscheinen, besonders deutlich auf und markiere die Schwierigkeiten farblich.

Pick-up C In town

map [mæp]	Stadtplan, Landkarte
of [ɒv; əv]	von
museum [mju:'zi:əm]	Museum
river ['rɪvə]	Fluss
bridge [brɪdʒ]	Brücke
information centre [ˌɪnfə'meɪʃn 'sentə]	Touristeninformation
information *(no pl.)* [ˌɪnfə'meɪʃn]	Information, Informationen
police station [pə'li:s ˌsteɪʃn]	Polizeirevier, Polizeiwache
police [pə'li:s]	Polizei
bus stop ['bʌs ˌstɒp]	Bushaltestelle
castle ['kɑ:sl]	Burg, Schloss
sweet shop ['swi:t ˌʃɒp]	Süßwarenladen
church [tʃɜ:tʃ]	Kirche
place [pleɪs]	Ort
near [nɪə]	nahe, in der Nähe von
opposite ['ɒpəzɪt]	gegenüber
to **get to** ['get tə]	kommen zu, kommen nach, erreichen
Excuse me. [ɪk'skju:s mi]	Entschuldigung. / Entschuldigen Sie.
to **go down** [gəʊ 'daʊn]	hinuntergehen; entlanggehen
down [daʊn]	herunter, hinunter, nach unten, hinab
to **turn right** [ˌtɜ:n 'raɪt]	(nach) rechts abbiegen
to **turn** [tɜ:n]	einbiegen, abbiegen
right [raɪt]	rechte/-r/-s; rechts

left [left]	linke/-r/-s; links
straight on [streɪt‿'ɒn]	geradeaus
straight [streɪt]	gerade(aus); direkt
to **cross** [krɒs]	überqueren, über … gehen
on your right/left [ɒn jə 'raɪt, 'left]	rechts / links, auf der rechten / linken Seite
on his way [ˌɒn hɪz 'weɪ]	auf dem Weg, unterwegs

Unit 4 Greenwich Project Week

Check-in

to **work** [wɜ:k]	arbeiten
interesting ['ɪntrəstɪŋ]	interessant
sights *(pl.)* [saɪts]	Sehenswürdigkeiten
tourist ['tʊərɪst]	Tourist, Touristin
brochure ['brəʊʃə]	Broschüre
Underground ['ʌndəgraʊnd]	U-Bahn
train [treɪn]	Zug
station ['steɪʃn]	Station, Bahnhof
young [jʌŋ]	jung
here [hɪə]	hierher, hierhin
tunnel ['tʌnl]	Tunnel
to **go** [gəʊ]	führen
world [wɜ:ld]	Welt
line [laɪn]	Linie; Zeile
Greenwich Mean Time (= **GMT**) [ˌgrenɪdʒ 'mi:n ˌtaɪm]	westeuropäische Zeit
visitor ['vɪzɪtə]	Besucher, Besucherin
foot pl. **feet** [fʊt; fi:t]	Fuß
west [west]	Westen
east [i:st]	Osten
hour [aʊə]	Stunde
too much [tu: 'mʌtʃ]	zu viel
North Sea [ˌnɔ:θ 'si:]	Nordsee
north [nɔ:θ]	Norden
sea [si:]	Meer, die See

to **call** [kɔ:l]	nennen
wonder [ˈwʌndə]	Wunder
famous [ˈfeɪməs]	berühmt
ship [ʃɪp]	Schiff
life pl. **lives** [laɪf; laɪvz]	Leben
from all round the world [frəm‿ˈɔ:l ˌraʊnd ðə ˈwɜ:ld]	aus aller Welt
to **go with** [gəʊ ˈwɪð]	passen zu, gehören zu
part [pɑ:t]	Teil

Language 1: Transport in Greenwich

finding the way [ˌfaɪndɪŋ ðə ˈweɪ]	den Weg finden
transport *(no pl.)* [ˈtrænspɔ:t]	Verkehrsmittel, Beförderung
all [ɔ:l]	alle/-s; ganz
by (Underground) [baɪ]	mit (der U-Bahn), per
driver [ˈdraɪvə]	Fahrer, Fahrerin
to **catch** [kætʃ]	nehmen *(Bus, Zug)*
to **drive** [draɪv]	fahren
taxi [ˈtæksi]	Taxi
special [ˈspeʃl]	besondere/-r/-s
to **get** [get]	holen, bringen; bekommen
to **speak (to)** [spi:k tə]	sprechen (mit)
pronoun [ˈprəʊnaʊn]	Pronomen, Fürwort
class [klɑ:s]	(Schul-)Klasse
to **give** [gɪv]	geben; schenken
everything [ˈevriθɪŋ]	alles
jumbled [ˈdʒʌmbld]	durcheinander geraten, vermischt
to **ask for ...** [ˈɑ:sk fə]	nach ... fragen
communication skills [kəˌmju:nɪˈkeɪʃn ˌskɪlz]	Sprechfertigkeiten, Kommunikationsfertigkeiten
to **repeat** [rɪˈpi:t]	wiederholen
of course [əv ˈkɔ:s]	natürlich, selbstverständlich

Language 2: I don't know!

I don't know! [ˌaɪ dəʊnt ˈnəʊ]	Ich weiß (es) nicht!
kid [kɪd]	Kind, Jugendlicher, Jugendliche
to **park** [pɑ:k]	parken
to **write down** [raɪt ˈdaʊn]	aufschreiben
to **give tours** [gɪv ˈtʊəz]	Stadtrundfahrten leiten
first [fɜ:st]	erste/-r/-s
How many … ? [haʊ ˈmeni]	Wie viele … ?
You've got me there! [jʊv ˌgɒt mi ˈðeə]	Da habt ihr mich kalt erwischt!
public [ˈpʌblɪk]	öffentlich
boat [bəʊt]	Boot, Schiff
to **think** [θɪŋk]	(nach)denken, finden, glauben

Language 3: The does-game

to **end** [end]	enden
test [test]	Test, Prüfung
best [best]	beste/-r/-s
to **win** [wɪn]	gewinnen
prize [praɪz]	Preis, Gewinn
easy-peasy [ˌi:ziˈpi:zi]	babyleicht
to **sell** [sel]	verkaufen
Me? [mi:; mi]	Ich?
silly [ˈsɪli]	Dummkopf
last [lɑ:st]	letzte/-r/-s
market [ˈmɑ:kɪt]	Markt
Make up your mind! [ˌmeɪk‿ˈʌp jə ˈmaɪnd]	Entscheide dich!
dear [dɪə]	Schatz
flower [flaʊə]	Blume
cheese [tʃi:z]	Käse
to **guess** [ges]	(er)raten; vermuten

Language 4: The Greenwich test

question word ['kwestʃən ˌwɜ:d]	Fragewort
to **mean** [mi:n]	bedeuten; meinen
fast [fɑ:st]	schnell
to **correct** [kə'rekt]	korrigieren, berichtigen
winner ['wɪnə]	Gewinner, Gewinnerin
swimming pool ['swɪmɪŋ ˌpu:l]	Schwimmbad, Schwimmbecken

Text: Captain Terry and the pirates

captain ['kæptɪn]	Kapitän
pirate ['paɪrət]	Pirat, Seeräuber
wheel [wi:l]	Steuerrad, Steuer, Rad
that [ðæt; ðət]	dass
mate [meɪt]	(Schiffs)offizier; Freund, Freundin
crow's nest ['krəʊz ˌnest]	Ausguck, Krähennest
tea [ti:]	Tee
treasure map ['treʒə ˌmæp]	Schatzkarte
island ['aɪlənd]	Insel
bang [bæŋ]	Knall, Schlag
to **want** [wɒnt]	wollen, mögen
to **sail** [seɪl]	segeln
to **walk the plank** [ˌwɔ:k ðə 'plæŋk]	über eine Schiffsplanke ins Wasser getrieben werden *(alte Strafe für Seeleute)*
to **hurry up** [ˌhʌri 'ʌp]	sich beeilen
to **fight** [faɪt]	kämpfen; sich streiten
She runs all round him. [ʃi ˌrʌnz ɔ:l 'raʊnd hɪm]	Sie rennt um ihn herum.
to **lick** [lɪk]	(ab)lecken
to **act** [ækt]	spielen

Wordwise

every ten minutes alle zehn Minuten
[ˌevri ten 'mɪnɪts]

Check-out

He takes us everywhere. Er bringt uns überallhin.
[hi ˌteɪks‿əs‿'evriweə]

1 In town

Welche Gebäude und Orte gibt es in einer Stadt?

church, ______________________________

____

____

2 Opposites

Wie lautet das Gegenteil?

1. left ↔ ______________
2. old ↔ ______________
3. east ↔ ______________
4. to take ↔ ______________

3 Where are the houses?

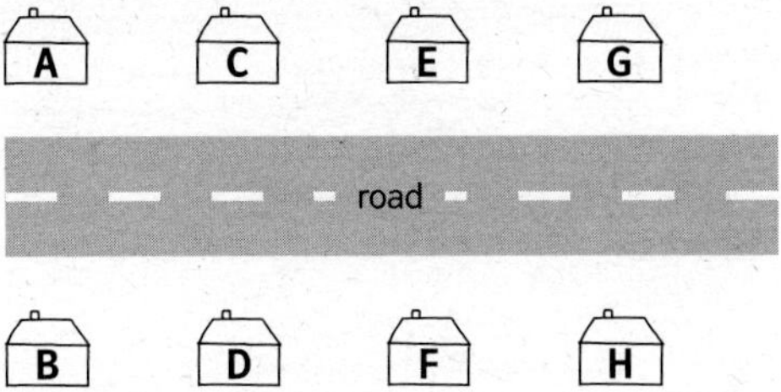

1. A is ______________________________ B.
2. E is ______________________________ C and G.
3. D is ______________________________ of B.
4. F is ______________________________ of H.

4 Transport

Vervollständige das Wortnetz.

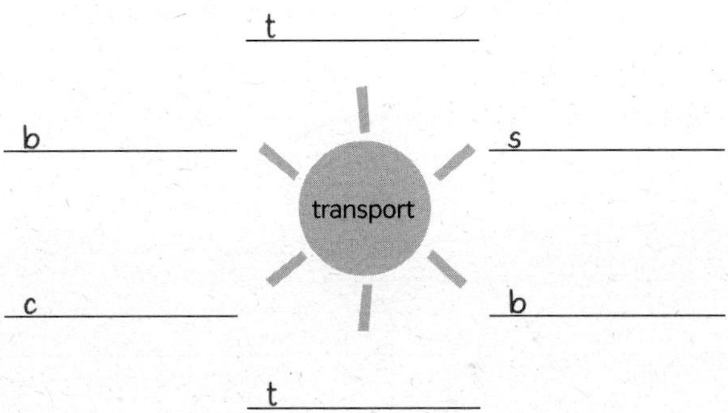

5 Which way?

6 Verbs

Wie viele Verben der Fortbewegung kennst du schon? Nenne mindestens vier.

____

____

7 Just one minute!

Schau dir die Wörter der Unit eine Minute lang an und schreibe danach alle Wörter / Ausdrücke auf, an die du dich erinnerst. Überprüfe anschließend die Rechtschreibung.

____

____

____

____

8 Finding the way

Ergänze die Objektformen der Personalpronomen.

1. mir: Can you tell ________ the way to the centre, please?
2. ihn: Sorry, I can't. Why don't you ask ________?
3. ihr: Can you give ________ the map, please?
4. es: Excuse me, where is Long Road? I can't find ________.
5. uns: Maybe the taxi driver can help ________.
6. euch: I can drive ________ there.
7. sie: Jane and Paul? We can meet ________ at the museum.

9 Words for pictures

Was ist abgebildet?

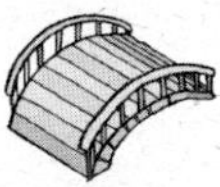

1. ____________________

2. ____________________

3. ____________________

4. ____________________

5. ____________________

10 Questions

Wie heißen diese Fragewörter auf Englisch?

1. Wer? ____________________ 4. Wo? ____________________

2. Was? ____________________ 5. Wie? ____________________

3. Wann? ____________________ 6. Warum? ____________________

11 Verbs

Welche Verben verstecken sich im Buchstabensalat? Notiere sie.

1. IWN to ____________________
2. CERCTOR to ____________________
3. SSUGE to ____________________
4. HKTNI to ____________________
5. AHCTC to ____________________

12 Captain Terry and the pirates

Kannst du zehn neue Wörter aus der Geschichte finden? Sie sind vertikal, horizontal und diagonal in beide Leserichtungen (vorwärts und rückwärts) versteckt.

F	P	I	R	A	T	E	J	A
S	I	O	A	M	R	P	G	L
L	S	G	E	Y	E	A	T	N
B	A	M	H	L	A	I	E	I
R	V	B	I	T	S	E	A	A
C	Q	A	L	R	U	S	I	T
K	S	H	I	P	R	I	O	P
O	H	I	L	E	E	H	W	A
R	I	S	L	A	N	D	Q	C

13 Odd one out

Welches Wort tanzt aus der Reihe? Markiere es.

1. church — museum — river
2. east — opposite — north
3. train — bike — skateboard
4. water — sweets — spaghetti
5. to run — to mean — to walk
6. team — beautiful — interesting

14 *to eat → lunch → sandwich*

An welche Vokabeln aus Units 1–4 denkst du, wenn du folgende Wörter liest?

town → ______________________

____

____

flat → ______________________

____

____

classroom → ______________________

____

____

weekend → ______________________

____

____

LERNTIPP

Fragt euch gegenseitig Vokabeln ab.

Unit 5 Birthday party

birthday party ['bɜːθdeɪ ˌpɑːti] Geburtstagsfeier
birthday ['bɜːθdeɪ] Geburtstag

Check-in

present ['preznt] Geschenk
size [saɪz] Größe
medium (M) ['miːdiəm] mittel(groß)
large (L) [lɑːdʒ] groß
extra large (XL) ['ekstrə ˌlɑːdʒ] besonders groß
How much is … ? ['haʊ mʌtʃ‿ɪz] Wie viel kostet … ?
It's two pounds. [ɪts ˌtuː 'paʊndz] Es kostet zwei Pfund.
to **buy** [baɪ] kaufen
newsagent ['njuːzˌeɪdʒnt] Zeitschriftengeschäft
clothes *(pl.)* [kləʊðz] Kleidung, Kleider
sports shop ['spɔːts ˌʃɒp] Sportgeschäft
money ['mʌni] Geld
penny pl. **pence** [peni; pens] Penny, Pence *(brit. Währungseinheit)*
to **go shopping** [gəʊ 'ʃɒpɪŋ] einkaufen gehen
assistant [ə'sɪstnt] Verkäufer/-in
expensive [ɪk'spensɪv] teuer

to **try on** [traɪ‿ˈɒn]	anprobieren
Here you are. [ˌhɪə ju‿ˈɑː]	Bitte schön.
customer [ˈkʌstəmə]	Kunde, Kundin

Language 1: Sam's invitation

date [deɪt]	Datum
invitation [ˌɪnvɪˈteɪʃn]	Einladung
the third of March [ðə ˌθɜːd‿əv ˈmɑːtʃ]	der dritte März
I'd like to ... (= I would like to) [aɪd ˈlaɪk tə]	ich möchte ... / ich würde gerne ...
I want to ... [aɪ ˈwɒnt tə]	ich möchte ... / ich will ...
to **invite ... out** [ɪnˌvaɪt ˈaʊt]	... (zu etwas) einladen
to **invite** [ɪnˈvaɪt]	einladen
pizza place [ˈpiːtsə ˌpleɪs]	Pizzeria
rich [rɪtʃ]	reich
Why don't you invite ... ? [waɪ dəʊnt jə ɪnˈvaɪt]	Warum lädst du nicht ... ein?
little [ˈlɪtl]	klein
cake [keɪk]	Kuchen, Torte
to **text** [tekst]	eine SMS schicken
right now [raɪt ˈnaʊ]	jetzt, sofort, gerade
man pl. **men** [mæn; men]	Mann
month [mʌnθ]	Monat
CU [ˈsiː juː]	bis bald *(Abkürzung in SMS oder E-Mail)*

Months

January [ˈdʒænjʊri] – Januar	**July** [dʒʊlˈaɪ] – Juli
February [ˈfebrʊri] – Februar	**August** [ˈɔːgəst] – August
March [mɑːtʃ] – März	**September** [sepˈtembə] – September
April [ˈeɪprl] – April	**October** [ɒkˈtəʊbə] – Oktober
May [meɪ] – Mai	**November** [nəʊˈvembə] – November
June [dʒuːn] – Juni	**December** [dɪˈsembə] – Dezember

Language 2: Shopping for Sam's birthday

using the present progressive ['ju:zɪŋ ðə ˌpreznt prə'gresɪv]	das *present progressive* benutzen
department store [dɪ'pɑ:tmənt ˌstɔ:]	Kaufhaus
just [dʒʌst]	gerade (eben), soeben
to **dance** [dɑ:ns]	tanzen
to **look for** ['lʊk fə]	suchen (nach)
still [stɪl]	noch, immer noch
thief pl. **thieves** [θi:f; θi:vz]	Dieb, Diebin
to **sing** [sɪŋ]	singen
the others [ði‿'ʌðəz]	die anderen

Language 3: The birthday cake

little ['lɪtl]	wenig
before [bɪ'fɔ:]	bis (zu), vor
lots of ['lɒts‿əv]	viel/-e, jede Menge
recipe ['resɪpi]	Rezept
How much ...? [haʊ 'mʌtʃ]	Wie viel ...?
sugar ['ʃʊgə]	Zucker
to **need** [ni:d]	brauchen
egg [eg]	Ei
to **want to know** [ˌwɒnt tə 'nəʊ]	wissen wollen
to **have fun** [hæv 'fʌn]	Spaß haben, sich amüsieren
a bag of ... [ə 'bæg‿əv]	eine Tüte ...
a box of ... [ə 'bɒks‿əv]	eine Schachtel ..., ein Karton ...
a few [ə 'fju:]	ein paar, einige; wenige
to **break** [breɪk]	(zer)brechen, kaputtgehen
flour [flaʊə]	Mehl
many ['meni]	viele
cook [kʊk]	Koch, Köchin
to **laugh** [lɑ:f]	lachen
a little [ə 'lɪtl]	ein wenig, etwas
candle ['kændl]	Kerze
in the world [ɪn ðə 'wɜ:ld]	auf der Welt

to **count** [kaʊnt]	zählen
a cup of [ə ˈkʌp‿əv]	eine Tasse …
chocolate crispies *(pl.)* [ˈtʃɒklət ˌkrɪspɪz]	Schokoplätzchen
to **go up** [gəʊ ˈʌp]	nach oben gehen
to **go down** [gəʊ ˈdaʊn]	nach unten gehen

Text: Happy birthday, Sam!

reading a story [ˈriːdɪŋ ə ˈstɔːri]	eine Geschichte lesen
title [ˈtaɪtl]	Titel
Happy Birthday! [ˌhæpi ˈbɜːθdeɪ]	Alles Gute zum Geburtstag!
ready [ˈredi]	fertig, bereit
to **be late for school** [bi ˌleɪt fə ˈskuːl]	zu spät zur Schule kommen
suddenly [ˈsʌdnli]	plötzlich, auf einmal
alarm clock [əˈlɑːm ˌklɒk]	Wecker
excited [ɪkˈsaɪtɪd]	aufgeregt, begeistert
surprise [səˈpraɪz]	Überraschung
karaoke machine [ˌkæriˈəʊki məˈʃiːn]	Karaokegerät
everyone [ˈevriwʌn]	jeder
even [ˈiːvn]	sogar, selbst
loud [laʊd]	laut
to **jump** [dʒʌmp]	springen
What's that song? [wɒts ðæt ˈsɒŋ]	Was ist das für ein Lied?
radio [ˈreɪdiəʊ]	Radio
Don't you listen to the radio? [dəʊnt jə ˌlɪsn tə ðə ˈreɪdiəʊ]	Hörst du kein Radio?
to **live** [lɪv]	wohnen, leben
radio station [ˈreɪdiəʊ ˌsteɪʃn]	Radiosender
to **take notes** [teɪk ˈnəʊts]	sich Notizen machen
heading [ˈhedɪŋ]	Überschrift, Titel

Wordwise

finding words [ˌfaɪndɪŋ ˈwɜːdz] Wörter finden
dictionary [ˈdɪkʃnri] Wörterbuch
alphabetical [ˌælfəˈbetɪkl] alphabetisch
etc. (= **et cetera**) [ɪtˈsetrə] usw. (= und so weiter)

1 Sizes

Wie groß ist das T-Shirt?

1. ______________________________

2. ______________________________

3. ______________________________

4. ______________________________

2 Matching words

Welche Wörter passen zusammen? Verbinde sie.

assistant	penny
birthday	large
pound	men
small	customer
man	present

3 Months 1

An welche Monate denkst du, wenn du die folgenden Bilder siehst? Notiere die Monatsnamen.

1. ____________________ 2 ____________________

3. ____________________ 4. ____________________

5. ____________________ 6. ____________________

4 Months 2

Notiere die in Übung 3 fehlenden Monate.

____________________ ____________________

____________________ ____________________

____________________ ____________________

5 Missing words

Welches Wort fehlt?

1. first, second, ____________________
2. ____________________, May, June
3. small, ____________________, large
4. day, week, ____________________
5. ____________________, nineteenth, twentieth
6. a bag of, a box of, a p____________________ of

6 Present progressive

Schreibe die Verlaufsform der Verben auf.

1. I win → I am ____________________
2. he looks → he is ____________________
3. she puts → she is ____________________
4. they dance → they are ____________________
5. you write → you are ____________________
6. we listen → we are ____________________

7 Shopping list

Was musst du einkaufen?

1. 

2. 

3. 

4. 

5. 

6. 

1. one bag of ______________________.
2. one _______ of ________________.
3. one _______ of ________________.
4. some ______________________.
5. a bag of ____________________.
6. two ______________ of __________.

8 *Much* or *many*?

1. How __________________ eggs? Ten eggs.
2. How __________________ sugar? One bag.
3. How __________________ flour? One bag.
4. How __________________ sandwiches? Four sandwiches.
5. How __________________ is the chocolate? It's 49 p.

9 Little words

Kennst du die englische Übersetzung?

1. ein paar, einige ______________________
2. sogar, selbst ______________________
3. zurück ______________________
4. noch, immer noch ______________________

10 Word snake

In der Schlange sind neun Verben aus der Unit versteckt. Markiere sie zunächst und übersetze sie anschließend.

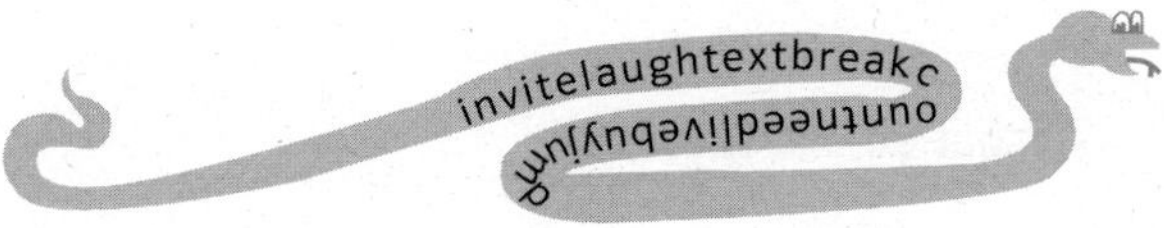

____

____

____

____

____

____

____

11 Words for pictures

Wie heißen die Dinge?

1. ______________________

2. ______________________

3. ______________________

4. ______________________

5. ______________________

12 What do you say?

Was sagst du, wenn …

1. … du wissen möchtest, was der Stadtplan kostet.

____

2. … du einen Apfel möchtest.

____

3. … du fragen möchtest, wie viele CDs jemand hat.

____

4. … du fragst, ob du jemandem helfen kannst.

____

LERNTIPP

Bilde Wortnetze.

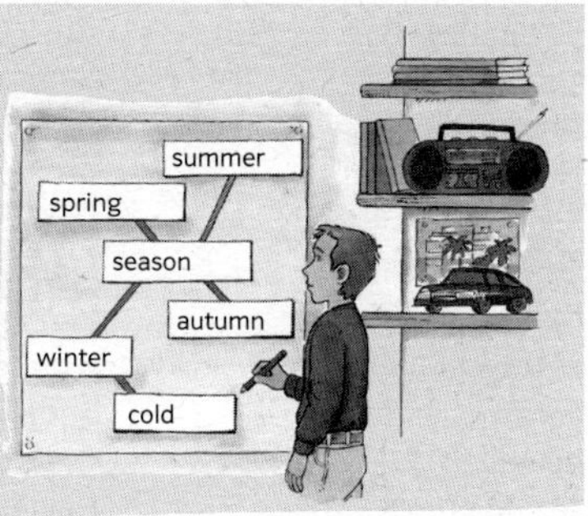

Unit 6 Beach holiday

Check-in

beach holiday ['bi:tʃ ˌhɒlədeɪ]	Strandurlaub
holiday(s) ['hɒlədeɪ; 'hɒlədeɪz]	Ferien, Urlaub
mile [maɪl]	Meile
from [frɒm; frəm]	von … entfernt
Britain ['brɪtn]	Großbritannien
east of ['i:st‿əv]	östlich von
a pier a mile long [ə 'pɪə ə ˌmaɪl 'lɒŋ]	ein Pier, der eine Meile lang ist
arcade games *(pl.)* [ɑ:'keɪd ˌgeɪmz]	Spielautomaten
in the town of Penzance [ɪn ðə 'taʊn‿əv pen'zæns]	in der Stadt Penzance
warm [wɔ:m]	warm
to **go surfing** [gəʊ 'sɜ:fɪŋ]	surfen gehen
wave [weɪv]	Welle, Woge
kite festival ['kaɪt ˌfestɪvl]	Drachenfest
to **fly a kite** [flaɪ ə 'kaɪt]	einen Drachen steigen lassen
to **fly** [flaɪ]	fliegen
winter ['wɪntə]	Winter

cold [kəʊld]	kalt
coast [kəʊst]	Küste
summer ['sʌmə]	Sommer
mountain ['maʊntɪn]	Berg
to **climb** [klaɪm]	(hinauf)steigen, hinaufklettern, erklimmen
village ['vɪlɪdʒ]	Dorf
lighthouse ['laɪthaʊs]	Leuchtturm
windy ['wɪndi]	windig
south [saʊθ]	Süden
ocean ['əʊʃn]	Ozean
seaside town [ˌsi:saɪd 'taʊn]	Küstenstadt

Language 1: Penzance

planning your holidays [ˌplænɪŋ jə 'hɒlədeɪz]	den Urlaub planen
to **surf on the Internet** [ˌsɜ:f‿ɒn ði‿'ɪntənet]	im Internet surfen
harbour ['hɑ:bə]	Hafen
meal [mi:l]	Mahlzeit, Essen
restaurant ['restrɑ:ŋ]	Restaurant, Gaststätte
season ['si:zn]	Jahreszeit; Saison
autumn ['ɔ:təm]	Herbst
spring [sprɪŋ]	Frühling
family fun ['fæmli ˌfʌn]	Spaß für die ganze Familie
to **click on** ['klɪk‿ɒn]	anklicken
to **build** [bɪld]	bauen
sand castle ['sænd ˌkɑ:sl]	Sandburg
ice-cream [ˌaɪs'kri:m]	Eiscreme, Eis
must [mʌst]	müssen
to **pack** [pæk]	(ein)packen
welly pl. **wellies** ['weli; weliz]	Gummistiefel
rain [reɪn]	Regen
swimsuit ['swɪmsu:t]	Badeanzug
sunglasses *(pl.)* ['sʌnˌglɑ:sɪz]	Sonnenbrille
address book [ə'dres ˌbʊk]	Adressbuch
postcard ['pəʊskɑ:d]	Postkarte

to **think of** ['θɪŋk‿əv]	halten von, denken über
over there [ˌəʊvə 'ðeə]	(nach) dort drüben

Language 2: On the beach

present progressive [ˌpreznt prə'gresɪv]	Verlaufsform des Präsens / der Gegenwart
on the beach [ɒn ðə 'biːtʃ]	am Strand
to **ruin** ['ruːɪn]	zerstören, ruinieren
safe [seɪf]	sicher, ungefährlich
alone [ə'ləʊn]	allein
thanks a lot [ˌθæŋks‿ə 'lɒt]	vielen Dank
Hooray! [hʊ'reɪ]	Hurra!
tooth pl. **teeth** [tuːθ; tiːθ]	Zahn
doghouse ['dɒghaʊs]	Hundehütte
signal word ['sɪgnl ˌwɜːd]	Signalwort
to **have breakfast** [hæv 'brekfəst]	frühstücken
this morning [ðɪs 'mɔːnɪŋ]	heute Morgen

Language 3: Some souvenirs of Penzance

some [sʌm]	einige, ein paar; etwas
any ['enɪ]	irgendein/-e/-er; irgendwelche
souvenir [ˌsuːvn'ɪə]	Andenken, Souvenir
in here [ɪn 'hiːə]	hier drin
mug [mʌg]	Becher
to **take off** [teɪk‿'ɒf]	abnehmen, ausziehen, herunternehmen
shelf pl. **shelves** [ʃelf; ʃelvz]	Regal, Regalbrett
I don't like them. [aɪ dəʊnt 'laɪk ˌðəm]	Sie gefallen mir nicht.
to **keep** [kiːp]	behalten, aufbewahren
pair [peə]	Paar
another [ə'nʌðə]	noch ein/-e; ein/-e andere/-r/-s
to **wait for** ['weɪt fə]	warten auf

cheap [tʃi:p]	billig, preiswert
on the way home [ˌɒn ðe weɪ ˈhəʊm]	auf dem Weg nach Hause
sweets *(pl.)* [swi:ts]	Süßigkeiten
not even [nɒt ˈi:vn]	(noch) nicht einmal

Text: Grace Darling's adventure

adventure [ədˈventʃə]	Abenteuer
to **read to** [ri:d ˈtə]	jmdm. vorlesen
storm [stɔ:m]	Sturm, Unwetter, Gewitter
to **rain** [reɪn]	regnen
to **pitter-patter** [ˈpɪtəˌpætə]	prasseln, klopfen, trappeln
strong [strɒŋ]	stark, kräftig
wind [wɪnd]	Wind
rock [rɒk]	Fels, Riff, Stein
to **crash** [kræʃ]	aufprallen, zusammenstoßen
at once [ət ˈwʌns]	auf einmal; sofort
stormy [ˈstɔ:mi]	stürmisch
against [əˈgenst]	gegen
to **sink** [sɪŋk]	untergehen, sinken
great [greɪt]	groß, riesig
to **row** [rəʊ]	rudern
out [aʊt]	heraus, hinaus, nach draußen
to **be scared for** [bi ˈskeəd fə]	Angst haben um
scared [skeəd]	verängstigt
will [wɪl]	Wille
to **hear** [hɪə]	hören
Don't worry. [dəʊnt ˈwʌri]	Mach dir keine Sorgen.
to **get into** [get‿ˈɪntə]	(ein)steigen
that day [ðæt ˈdeɪ]	an jenem Tag
to **die** [daɪ]	sterben
to **survive** [səˈvaɪv]	überleben
to **retell** [ri:ˈtel]	nacherzählen; nochmals erzählen

on a train [ɒn‿ə ˈtreɪn]	im Zug
to **think about** [θɪŋk‿əˈbaʊt]	halten von, denken über

Wordwise

noun [naʊn]	Nomen, Hauptwort
verb [vɜ:b]	Verb, Zeitwort
to **look up** [lʊk‿ˈʌp]	nachschlagen, nachschauen
woman pl. **women** [ˈwʊmən; ˈwɪmɪn]	Frau
person pl. **people** [ˈpɜ:sn; pi:pl]	Person, Mensch
fish pl. **fish** [fɪʃ]	Fisch
scarf pl. **scarves** [skɑ:f; skɑ:vz]	Schal, Tuch

Check-out

Oops! [u:ps]	Hoppla!

1 Missing letters

Wie heißt das Wort? Ergänze die fehlenden Buchstaben.

1. f ___ s t i ___ a l
2. b ___ ___ c h
3. m o ___ n t ___ ___ n
4. ___ ___ l l a g e
5. l i ___ h t h ___ ___ s e
6. s ___ ___ d c a s ___ l ___

2 Numbers and dates

a) *Schreibe die Zahlen in Ziffern auf.*

1. one thousand two hundred and seven → ____________
2. sixty-six thousand three hundred and fifty-five

   → ____________
3. eight hundred and eighty-eight thousand four hundred

   and twenty-one → ____________

b) *Schreibe die Jahreszahlen in Worten aus.*

1. 1900 → ____

   ____
2. 1742 → ____

   ____
3. 2008 → ____

   ____

3 Weather

Schau dir die Bilder an. Notiere Wörter, die das Wetter beschreiben.

1. 

2. 

______________________ ______________________

______________________ ______________________

______________________ ______________________

4 *bring* or *take*?

1. Can we ____________ our dog to the beach?
2. Please ____________ me my sunglasses.
3. Where is my Discman? I must ____________ it, too.
4. Let's ____________ grandma a nice present!

5 Seasons

Wie heißen die vier Jahreszeiten?

6 Odd one out

Welches Wort tanzt aus der Reihe? Markiere es.

1. kite	wind	rain
2. to go surfing	to go swimming	to go on holiday
3. meal	restaurant	swimsuit
4. wave	harbour	ocean
5. to pack	to climb	to fly
6. cold	warm	safe

7 Souvenirs

Welche Andenken kannst du aus dem Urlaub mitbringen?

1. ______________________________

2. ______________________________

3. ______________________________

4. ______________________________

5. ______________________________

6. ______________________________

8 Plurals

Wie lautet der Plural?

1. tooth – ______________
2. man – ______________
3. child – ______________
4. woman – ______________
5. mouse – ______________
6. thief – ______________
7. fish – ______________
8. scarf – ______________
9. family – ______________
10. shelf – ______________
11. foot – ______________
12. person – ______________

9 Long words

Verbinde die deutschen Ausdrücke mit der richtigen Übersetzung.

1. Angst haben um	a) to have breakfast
2. Mach dir keine Sorgen!	b) to be scared for
3. frühstücken	c) to think of
4. auf einmal; sofort	d) Don't worry!
5. halten von, denken über	e) over there
6. dort drüben	f) at once

10 New words

Diese Wörter fand ich in Unit 6 besonders …

schwer zu merken	schwer auszusprechen	nützlich

LERNTIPP

Bring Bewegung ins Lernen! Geh beim Vokabellernen auf und ab!

Unit 7 Animals in the city

Check-in

animal ['ænɪml]	Tier
city ['sɪti]	Großstadt
wild [waɪld]	wild
fox [fɒks]	Fuchs
bird [bɜ:d]	Vogel
zoo [zu:]	Zoo
monkey ['mʌŋki]	Affe
farm [fɑ:m]	Bauernhof
field [fi:ld]	Wiese, Weide, Acker
at the same time [ət ðə ˌseɪm 'taɪm]	zur selben Zeit, gleichzeitig
chicken ['tʃɪkɪn]	Huhn; Hähnchen, Hühnchen
pig [pɪg]	Schwein
cow [kaʊ]	Kuh
sheep pl. **sheep** [ʃi:p]	Schaf
horse [hɔ:s]	Pferd
farmhand ['fɑ:mhænd]	Landarbeiter, Landarbeiterin
schools officer ['sku:lz ˌɒfɪsə]	*hier:* Beauftragter / Beauftragte für Schulklassen

activity [æk'tɪvəti]	Aktivität
already [ɔ:l'redi]	schon, bereits

Language 1: On the farm

duty ['dju:ti]	Pflicht
class trip [ˌklɑ:s 'trɪp]	Klassenfahrt, Klassenausflug
to **milk** [mɪlk]	melken
to **look after** [lʊk‿'ɑ:ftə]	sich kümmern um; aufpassen auf
grass [grɑ:s]	Gras
mustn't ['mʌsnt]	nicht dürfen
nervous ['nɜ:vəs]	nervös, aufgeregt
calm [kɑ:m]	ruhig, friedlich
allergic to [ə'lɜ:dʒɪk tə]	allergisch auf
shed [ʃed]	Stall
Pooh! [pu:]	Igitt!
to **stink** [stɪŋk]	stinken
to **muck out** [mʌk‿'aʊt]	ausmisten
bacon ['beɪkn]	(Schinken)speck
four of them ['fɔ:r‿əv ðəm]	vier davon *(Personen, Tiere …)*
milk [mɪlk]	Milch
bottle ['bɒtl]	Flasche
to **fight over** [faɪt‿'əʊvə]	sich streiten um
hand [hænd]	Hand

Language 2: Cyberpets

looking after a pet [ˌlʊkɪŋ ˌɑ:ftər‿ə 'pet]	sich um ein Tier kümmern
cyberpet ['saɪbəpet]	virtuelles Haustier
should [ʃʊd]	sollte/-est/-en/-et
owner ['əʊnə]	Besitzer, Besitzerin
to **choose** [tʃu:z]	(aus)wählen
ear [ɪə]	Ohr
from time to time [frəm ˌtaɪm tə 'taɪm]	von Zeit zu Zeit
holiday home ['hɒlədeɪ ˌhəʊm]	*hier:* Tierpension

bad [bæd]	schlecht; böse
word order ['wɜ:d‿ɔ:də]	Wortstellung, Satzstellung
subject ['sʌbdʒɪkt]	Subjekt, Satzgegenstand
object ['ɒbdʒɪkt]	Objekt, Satzergänzung
for (many) hours/years … [fə ˌmeni 'aʊəz; 'jɪəz]	stundenlang / jahrelang
what it looks like [ˌwɒt‿ɪt 'lʊks laɪk]	wie es aussieht

Language 3: TTS school magazine

competition [ˌkɒmpə'tɪʃn]	Wettbewerb
moment ['məʊmənt]	Moment, Augenblick
card [kɑ:d]	Chip, Speicherkarte (*für Digitalkameras*)
camera ['kæmrə]	Fotoapparat, Kamera
to **take a photo** [ˌteɪk‿ə 'fəʊtəʊ]	ein Foto machen
to **think of** ['θɪŋk‿əv]	(sich) ausdenken, sich etwas einfallen lassen

Text: Sam's new friend

one evening [wʌn‿'i:vnɪŋ]	eines Abends
garage ['gærɑ:ʒ]	Garage; Werkstatt; Tankstelle
to **run after** [rʌn‿'ɑ:ftə]	hinterherrennen
shock [ʃɒk]	Schock, Schreck
dark [dɑ:k]	dunkel
I know a fox when I see one! [aɪ ˌnəʊ ə 'fɒks wen‿aɪ 'si: wʌn]	Ich erkenne einen Fuchs sofort!
leg [leg]	Bein
vet [vet]	Tierarzt, Tierärztin
territory ['terɪtri]	Gebiet, Revier, Territorium
may [meɪ]	(vielleicht) können; dürfen
to **explain** [ɪk'spleɪn]	erklären
to **mend** [mend]	heilen; reparieren
to **smile** [smaɪl]	lächeln
bowl [bəʊl]	Schüssel
night [naɪt]	Nacht; Abend

worried ['wʌrɪd]	beunruhigt, besorgt
to **be right** [bɪ 'raɪt]	Recht haben
to **stand** [stænd]	stehen
sad [sæd]	traurig
empty ['emti]	leer
thanks to ['θæŋks tə]	dank (dir / Ihnen), wegen
dead [ded]	tot
if [ɪf]	wenn, falls; ob
to **drink** [drɪŋk]	trinken
clear [klɪə]	klar, verständlich

Wordwise

meaning ['mi:nɪŋ]	Bedeutung
in the street [ɪn ðə 'stri:t]	auf der Straße
next [nekst]	nächste/-r/-s
just now [ˌdʒʌst 'naʊ]	gerade, im Augenblick

1 What word?

Welches Wort verbirgt sich hinter der Lautschrift?

1. [fɑ:m] ________________
2. [mɪlk] ________________
3. [æk'tɪvəti] ________________
4. ['nɜ:vəs] ________________
5. ['əʊnə] ________________
6. [grɑ:s] ________________

2 Animals 1

Nenne die Tiere (Singular und Plural).

1. ______________________

____

2. ______________________

____

3. ______________________

____

4. ______________________

____

3 Animals 2

Sind diese Tiere Haustiere oder Bauernhoftiere? Einige Tiere können beiden Gruppen zugeordnet werden.

horse

cat cow sheep dog pig mouse

Pet	Farm
______________	______________
______________	______________
______________	______________
______________	______________

4 *must, needn't* or *mustn't*?

Wie kannst du die Aussagen anders formulieren?
Füge ***must, needn't*** *oder* ***mustn't*** *ein.*

1. Don't fight over who feeds the animals. You can take turns! – You ________________ fight over who feeds the animals. You can take turns!
2. Please be calm with the animals. – You ________________ be calm with the animals.
3. You don't want to muck out the pig shed? That's OK. – You ________________ muck out the pig shed.
4. It isn't nice to make the animals nervous. – You ________________ make the animals nervous.
5. Please collect the eggs in the morning. – You ________________ collect the eggs in the morning.
6. Don't eat the animals' food. – You ________________ eat the animals' food.

5 Word order

Formuliere je einen Satz mit diesen Wörtern.

1. to milk – farmhand – in the shed – every morning – cows

____

____

2. on Saturdays – with the animals – on the farm – children – to help

____

____

3. monkeys – after school – to visit – class – at the zoo

____

____

6 Little words

Wie heißen diese kleinen Wörter auf Englisch?

1. und ________________
2. aber ________________
3. wenn, falls ________________
4. oder ________________
5. weil, da ________________
6. also; so ________________
7. bevor ________________
8. wenn ________________

7 Verbs and nouns

Verbinde die Verben mit dem passenden Substantiv. Einige Substantive können mehreren Verben zugeordnet werden.

1. to look after	a) the ball
2. to fight over	b) a new idea
3. to take a photo of	c) a pet
4. to look up	d) a word
5. to think of	e) food
6. to run after	f) the sea

8 Adjectives

Welche neuen Adjektive hast du in Unit 7 gelernt? Notiere sie.

wild, ____________________________

____

____

9 What do you say?

Was sagst du, wenn …

1. … du jemandem deine Hilfe anbietest?

___

2. … du die Hilfe, die dir jemand anbietet, gerne annimmst?

___

3. … du die Hilfe, die dir jemand anbietet, dankend ablehnst?

___

10 Easy or not?

Schau dir sämtliche Wörter der Unit erneut an.
Notiere anschließend …

a) *… zwei Vokabeln, die dir leicht fallen.*

___

b) *… drei Vokabeln, die du dir nicht merken kannst.*

___

___

11 *birthday → to invite → present*

An welche Vokabeln aus Units 5–7 denkst du, wenn du folgende Wörter liest?

holiday → ______________________________

____

____

shopping → ______________________________

____

____

class trip → ______________________________

____

____

12 Green Line 1: Word search

Suche die folgenden Wörter aus Green Line 1 im Gitternetz. Sie sind vertikal, horizontal und diagonal in beide Leserichtungen (vorwärts und rückwärts) versteckt.

autumn	early	mum	surprise
basketball	funny	pair	that
birthday	have	park	then
brochure	hurry	place	throw
cow	language	purple	tip
cupboard	may	second	train
dictionary	more	smile	winter

F	I	D	B	A	S	K	E	T	B	A	L	L	E
H	M	F	K	U	M	D	F	H	I	T	Q	E	R
U	L	Q	S	T	I	R	T	A	R	R	V	N	U
T	T	E	U	U	L	A	H	T	T	A	M	T	H
J	S	M	U	M	E	O	R	L	H	I	W	O	C
O	E	N	T	N	O	B	O	P	D	N	S	E	O
S	C	G	K	R	A	P	W	I	A	Q	F	C	R
V	O	F	S	P	L	U	L	T	Y	I	H	R	B
G	N	W	O	A	S	C	A	O	R	X	R	K	P
X	D	I	C	T	I	O	N	A	R	Y	A	M	U
F	N	E	H	H	T	U	G	J	U	N	E	O	R
H	W	T	U	E	V	B	U	M	H	N	A	R	P
Z	N	V	A	N	X	Z	A	K	J	U	R	E	L
X	W	I	N	T	E	R	G	W	I	F	L	P	E
S	U	R	P	R	I	S	E	A	Y	Z	Y	B	C

[Trailer 1 Summer with the Taylors]

trailer [treɪlə]	Anhänger
past [pɑ:st]	Vergangenheit
dear [dɪə]	Lieber … , Liebe … *(Anrede in Briefen)*
yesterday ['jestədeɪ]	gestern
lake [leɪk]	See
love [lʌv]	Liebe Grüße, Herzliche Grüße (am Briefende)
irregular [ɪ'regjələ]	unregelmäßig
regular ['regjələ]	regelmäßig
trampolining ['træmpəli:nɪŋ]	Trampolin hüpfen

[Trailer 2 Old junk]

plan [plæn]	Plan
junk [dʒʌŋk]	Gerümpel, Abfall; Ramsch
to clear out [klɪə 'aʊt]	ausräumen; entrümpeln
bath [bɑ:θ]	Badewanne
nose [nəʊz]	Nase
mouth [maʊθ]	Mund

1 The simple past 1

Verbinde die passenden Verbformen.

1. to get	a) painted
2. to buy	b) ate
3. to stay	c) was / were
4. to find	d) got
5. to paint	e) had
6. to be	f) listened
7. to say	g) bought
8. to listen	h) found
9. to watch	i) said
10. to run	j) stayed
11. to eat	k) watched
12. to have	l) ran

2 The simple past 2

Füge das Verb in der richtigen Form ein.

1. Every day Carol sees her friend at the bus stop.

   Yesterday she ____________ her friend's brother, too.

2. We always go ice-skating in the winter.

   Last winter we ____________ skiing.

3. Mrs Green always comes home at 4 o'clock.

   Yesterday she ____________ home at 7 o'clock.

4. Hamida meets Sally at school.

   Last weekend she ____________ Sally at the swimming pool.

1 Food

1. Tom, the mouse, loves … .
2. Fish and …
3. Mmm, there is a bag of … in my schoolbag.
4. It's brown or white and it's sweet.
5. There are twelve candles on the birthday …
6. It's so hot today! Can we get …, please?
7. In England people eat … and eggs for breakfast.
8. I'd like my tea with milk and …, please.
9. I always eat a sandwich and an … for lunch.
10. Water, tea etc. = …
11. What does your cat eat? – Cat …!
12. … are sweet.
13. … comes from cows and is white.
14. Have you got a recipe for chocolate …?
15. … is my favourite pasta.

2 Word circle

Das nächste Wort fängt mit dem letzten Buchstaben des vorherigen Wortes an.

1. Grass is …
2. The opposite of day.
3. You sit on a chair at a …
4. You have two of them in your face.
5. The opposite of north.
6. 60 minutes = 1 …
7. bed…, bath…, living …
8. The plural of 'man' is …
9. I'm German. = My … is German.
10. This is my first … at the new school.
11. to … a bike, to … a horse
12. morning, afternoon, …, night

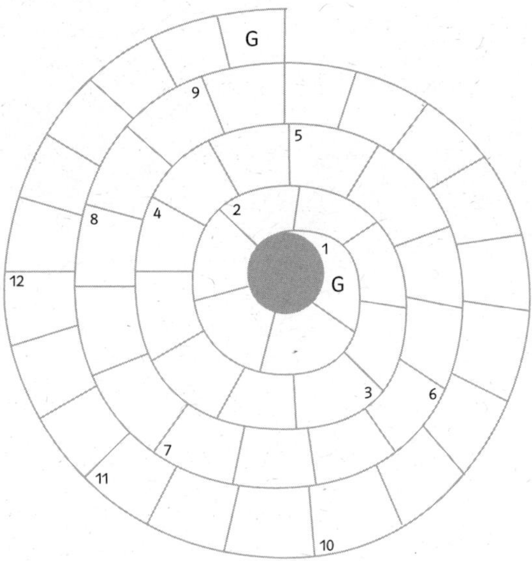

Lösungen

Unit 1

1 *Vorschlag:* Zur Begrüßung: Hi!, Hello!, Good morning! Zum Abschied: Goodbye!, Bye!

2 1. under 2. on 3. in 4. behind

3 1. What's your name? 2. How old are you? 3. Where are you from?

4 1. I am 2. you're 3. he is 4. she's 5. it is 6. we're 7. you are 8. they're

5 1. My name is … 2. I am … years old. 3. I am from … 4. My phone number is …

6 one, three, seven, five, eight, twelve, ten, nine, eleven, two, four, six

7 1. sixteen 2. twenty 3. twenty-seven 4. forty-two 5. eighty

8 *Deine eigenen Antworten*

9 1. What 2. Where 3. How 4. Who

10 1. ruler 2. pen 3. table 4. chair 5. exercise book 6. ball

11 *Vorschlag:* new, big, cool, nice, late, easy, boring, scary, favourite, terrible, polite

12 1. listen 2. write 3. spell 4. make 5. shout 6. fill in

13 1. an 2. a 3. an 4. a 5. an 6. a

14 1. window 2. cupboard 3. door 4. table 5. desk 6. chair

15 1. please 2. cool 3. pencil 4. letter

Pick-up A und Unit 2

1 1. blue 2. yellow 3. red 4. white

2 1. bathroom 2. bedroom 3. kitchen 4. living room

3 1. bed 2. table 3. computer 4. picture 5. sofa 6. cupboard

4 dad, mum, grandad, grandma, brother, sister

P	D	S	A	T	O	D	A
D	O	A	M	J	P	G	R
S	D	A	D	N	A	R	G
A	M	O	N	T	I	E	S
V	B	R	A	N	E	H	I
Q	F	L	R	L	S	T	S
H	P	M	G	B	I	O	T
A	U	J	P	Y	C	R	E
M	G	M	A	H	G	B	R

5 1. aunt 2. uncle 3. grandmother (grandma) 4. grandfather (grandad)

6 1. to stop 2. to close 3. downstairs 4. divorced from

7 1. Italian 2. Greek 3. Russian 4. Turkish 5. English 6. German

8 1. my 2. your 3. his 4. her 5. its 6. our 7. your 8. their

9 1. shed 2. T-shirt 3. magazine 4. drums

10 1. sprechen mit, reden mit 2. antworten, beantworten 3. beschreiben 4. erzählen; sagen 5. fragen 6. rufen, schreien 7. sagen 8. sprechen über

11 *Vorschlag:* tiny, funny, happy, small, good, great, not very good, nice, boring, busy, cool, silly, slow, new, beautiful

Pick-up B und Unit 3

1 Tuesday, Thursday, Saturday, Sunday

2 Monday, Wednesday, Friday

3 1. am 2. pm

4 minute, day, weekend, afternoon, today, evening, week

5 What time is it, please?

6 1. half past two 2. quarter past four 3. quarter to two 4. five past five 5. ten to eight 6. ten o'clock

7 sometimes, often, never, usually, always

8 *Vorschlag:* football, basketball, swimming, dancing

9 1. play 2. watches 3. goes 4. tells 5. ride 6. sing, dance

10 1. Was ist mit deinen / euren Hausaufgaben? 2. Wie geht es dir / euch / Ihnen? 3. Wie wär's mit Kino?

11 1. walks 2. goes 3. plays 4. watches

12 1. bike 2. guitar 3. clock 4. breakfast 5. drink

13 1. run 2. get / wake 3. fall 4. wake / get 5. get 6. fall

14 1. evening 2. throw 3. neighbour 4. story 5. hobby 6. orchestra 7. read 8. walk the dog

15 1. breakfast 2. today 3. to link 4. after 5. town 6. early

Link-up C und Unit 4

1 *Vorschlag:* museum, river, bridge, information centre, police station, bus stop, castle, cinema, park

2 1. right 2. young / new 3. west 4. to give

3 1. opposite 2. next to 3. on the right 4. on the left

4 train, ship, bus, taxi, car, bike

5 north, west, east, south

6 *Vorschlag:* to go, to walk, to run, to ride, to swim, to drive

7 *Deine eigenen Antworten*

8 1. me 2. him 3. her 4. it 5. us 6. you 7. them

9 1. bridge 3. skateboard 4. church 5. map 6. world

10 1. Who? 2. What? 3. When? 4. Where? 5. How? 6. Why?

11 1. win 2. correct 3. guess 4. think 5. catch

12 pirate, fight, treasure, eye, tea, sail, ship, wheel, island, captain

13 1. river 2. opposite 3. train 4. water 5. to mean 6. team

14 *Vorschlag:* town: bridge, bus stop, sweet shop, cinema, museum, …;
flat: living room, bedroom, bathroom, kitchen, bed, sofa, wardrobe, picture, …;
classroom: school, pupil, teacher, exercise book, diary, pencil, desk, chair, board, …;
weekend: football, basketball, to go swimming, to sleep, cinema, …

Unit 5

1 1. small 2. medium 3. large 4. extra large

2 assistant – customer, birthday – present, pound – penny, small – large, man – men

3 *Vorschlag*: 1. January 2. February 3. April 4. August 5. September 6. December

4 *Vorschlag*: March, May, June, July, October, November

5 1. third 2. April 3. medium 4. month 5. eighteenth 6. packet

6 1. winning 2. looking 3. putting 4. dancing 5. writing 6. listening

7 1. flour 2. box, eggs 3. bag, sugar 4. cheese 5. apples 6. tins, cat food

8 1. many 2. much 3. much 4. many 5. much

9 1. a few 2. even 3. back 4. still

10 to invite = einladen, to laugh = lachen, to text = eine SMS schicken, to break = (zer)brechen, kaputtgehen, to count = zählen, to need = brauchen, to live = wohnen, leben, to buy = kaufen, to jump = springen

11 1. present 2. money 3. alarm clock 4. cake 5. photo / picture

12 1. How much is the map? 2. I'd like an apple, please. 3. How many CDs have you got? 4. Can I help you?

Unit 6

1 1. festival 2. beach 3. mountain 4. village 5. lighthouse 6. sand castle

2 a) 1. 1,207 2. 66,355 3. 888,421
b) 1. nineteen hundred 2. seventeen fourty-two 3. two thousand and eight

3 *Vorschlag*: 1. cold, rain, wind, windy, stormy 2. warm, sun

4 1. take 2. bring 3. take 4. bring

5 spring, summer, autumn, winter

6 1. kite 2. to go on holiday 3. swimsuit 4. harbour 5. to pack 6. safe

7 1. postcards 2. mug 3. sweets 4. sunglasses 5. T-shirt 6. kite

8 1. teeth 2. men 3. children 4. women 5. mice 6. thieves 7. fish 8. scarves 9. families 10. shelves 11. feet 12. people

9 1. b), 2. d), 3. a), 4. f), 5. c), 6. e)
10 *Deine eigenen Antworten*

Unit 7

1 1. farm 2. milk 3. activity 4. nervous 5. owner 6. grass
2 1. pig, pigs 2. sheep, sheep 3. horse, horses 4. cow, cows
3 Pet: cat, dog, mouse; Farm: cow, sheep, pig, horse (cat, dog, mouse)
4 1. needn't 2. must 3. needn't 4. mustn't 5. must 6. mustn't
5 1. Every morning the farmhand milks the cows in the shed. / The farmhand milks the cows in the shed every morning 2. On Saturdays, children help with the animals on the farm. / Children help with the animals on the farm on Saturdays. 3. After school the class visits the monkeys at the zoo. / The class visits the monkeys at the zoo after school.
6 1. and 2. but 3. if 4. or 5. because 6. so 7. before 8. when
7 1. c), 2. a)/e), 3. c)/f), 4. d), 5. b), 6. a)/c)
8 nervous, calm, allergic to, bad, dark, worried, sad, empty, dead, clear
9 1. Can I … for you? / I can help you to … / Would you like some help with …? 2. Thanks, that's nice of you. / That's a big help. 3. Thanks, but I can do it. / That's OK. / You needn't help.
10 *Deine eigenen Antworten*
11 *Vorschlag:* holiday: beach, wave, sea, ocean, sun, surfing, warm, cold, coast, lighthouse, mountain, …; shopping: to buy, money, penny, pence, customer, assistant, clothes, sports shop, department store, expensive, to try on, newsagent, …;
class trip: zoo, farm, activity, …

12

F	I	D	B	A	S	K	E	T	B	A	L	L	E
H	M	F	K	U	M	D	F	H	I	T	Q	E	R
U	L	Q	S	T	I	R	T	A	R	R	V	N	U
T	T	E	U	U	L	A	H	T	T	A	M	T	H
J	S	M	U	M	E	O	R	L	H	I	W	O	C
O	E	N	T	N	O	B	O	P	D	N	S	E	O
S	C	G	K	R	A	P	W	I	A	Q	F	C	R
V	O	F	S	P	L	U	L	T	Y	I	H	R	B
G	N	W	O	A	S	C	A	O	R	X	R	K	P
X	D	I	C	T	I	O	N	A	R	Y	A	M	U
F	N	E	H	H	T	U	G	J	U	N	E	O	R
H	W	T	U	E	V	B	U	M	H	N	A	R	P
Z	N	V	A	N	X	Z	A	K	J	U	R	E	L
X	W	I	N	T	E	R	G	W	I	F	L	P	E
S	U	R	P	R	I	S	E	A	Y	Z	Y	B	C

[Trailer 1]

1 1. d), 2. g), 3. j), 4. h), 5. a), 6. c), 7. i), 8. f), 9. k), 10. l), 11. b), 12. e)

2 1. saw 2. went 3. came 4. met

Puzzles

1 1. cheese 2. chips 3. crisps 4. chocolate 5. cake 6. ice-cream 7. bacon 8. sugar 9. apple 10. drinks 11. food 12. sweets 13. milk 14. crispies 15. spaghetti

2 1. green 2. night 3. table 4. eyes 5. south 6. hour 7. room 8. men 9. nationality 10. year 11. ride 12. evening